COLUSA COUNTY FREE

Colusa County Free Library

3 0738 00031 2917

DATE DUE

GAYLORD 234			PRINTED IN U. S. A.

D0466653

C. 55226

Lord, Athena V.
   Pilot for spaceship earth; R. Buckminster
Fuller, architect, inventor, and poet.
Macmillan, c1978.
   168p. il. (JLG)

                              6-9   5c

   1. Fuller, Richard Buckminster, 1895-
2. Inventors. 3. Architects.

CUP
RLIN

NCC 99

PILOT FOR
SPACESHIP EARTH

C- 55226

x620.0092
Fuller
L

PILOT FOR
SPACESHIP EARTH

R. BUCKMINSTER FULLER,
Architect, Inventor, and Poet

ATHENA V. LORD

MACMILLAN PUBLISHING CO., INC.
New York

COLLIER MACMILLAN PUBLISHERS
London

COLUSA COUNTY FREE LIBRARY

The quotation by R. Buckminster Fuller on page 122 appeared in "In the Outlaw Area" by Calvin Tompkins (*The New Yorker*, January 8, 1966) and is reprinted by permission of *The New Yorker*.

The poem on page 136, "Environment" by Buckminster Fuller, Copyright 1972 by R. Buckminster Fuller, appeared in the December 1972 issue of *Architectural Design* Magazine, London, and is reprinted by permission of R. Buckminster Fuller and *Architectural Design*.

Picture Credits: All pictures except those on pages 52 and 128 were provided by courtesy of the R. Buckminster Fuller Archives and are reproduced with the permission of Mr. Fuller. The drawings on pages 53, 103 and 119 are by Christopher Kitrick; known photographic credits are: page 61, F. S. Lincoln; page 80, Arthur H. Linney; page 87, Kaufmann and Fabry; page 94, *Architectural Forum*; page 96, Ernest Weismann (*Architectural Forum*); page 116, Wayne F. Miller; page 144, Tom Monk.
    Page 52 (top), courtesy of Culver Pictures; page 52 (bottom), courtesy of Wide World Photos; page 128, courtesy of Christopher Lord.

Copyright © 1978 Athena V. Lord

All rights reserved. No part of this book may be reproduced or transmitted in any form or by any means, electronic or mechanical, including photocopying, recording or by any information storage and retrieval system, without permission in writing from the Publisher.

Macmillan Publishing Co., Inc.
866 Third Avenue, New York, N.Y. 10022
Collier Macmillan Canada, Ltd.

Printed in the United States of America

10   9   8   7   6   5   4   3   2   1

008839

LIBRARY OF CONGRESS CATALOGING IN PUBLICATION DATA

Lord, Athena V   Pilot for Spaceship Earth.

    Bibliography: p.   Includes index.

    SUMMARY: A biography of R. Buckminster Fuller, the architect and inventor whose investigations into the principles of nature influenced his designs and helped revolutionize our world.
    1. Fuller, Richard Buckminster, 1895–   —Juvenile literature.
2. Inventors—United States—Biography—Juvenile literature.
3. Architects—United States—Biography—Juvenile literature.
[1. Fuller, Richard Buckminster, 1895–   2. Inventors.
3. Architects]   I. Title.
T40.F86L67   620'.0092'4 [B] [92]   77-12629   ISBN 0-02-761420-4

For Victor, Sara, Christopher, Victoria,
and Alexandra, who all helped me, in James
Kavanaugh's words, "to begin to live the
rest of my life."

AUTHOR'S NOTE

In addition to library research, the material for this book was collected through interviews with friends and relatives, examination of public records, and attendance at Dr. Fuller's lectures in Buffalo and Philadelphia. I have consolidated details to convey the typical pattern of vacations on Bear Island. Wherever possible, I have tried to use Dr. Fuller's own words to describe a feeling, thought, or event.

I wish to express special thanks to Rosamond Kenison, Leslie and Dana Gibson, E. J. Applewhite, and Ada Pierce. With generosity and warm hospitality, they shared memories, corrected facts, and answered endless questions.

I also thank Lawrence L. Gross, Eileen C. Piazza, David F. Stephenson, and the Albany Public Library reference staff, who responded immediately to all calls for help; and especially my editor, Phyllis Larkin.

If there are any errors or inaccuracies in this account of the living legend that is R. Buckminster Fuller, the fault is mine. The whole was a labor of love.

Prologue

Push down, pull out, oars dipping, boat moving, the small boy in the rowboat pulled steadily toward the horseshoe-shaped harbor. Overhead, sea gulls wheeled and squawked as if to say he was not truly alone. He smiled. Other boys dreamed about the adventures to be had living on an island; Bucky Fuller lived them every summer. When Bucky was nine years old, his Grandma Andrews had been persuaded to buy an island in Maine. That next summer, the schooner *Polly* had brought the materials and men from Boston to build the large, shingled house that stood now on the high bluff of Bear Island.

Bucky jumped out of the rowboat and gave it a hard shove up onto the beach. He shivered once. The ice-cold waters of Penobscot Bay made a freezing carpet under his feet. At least his canvas shoes saved his feet from the spiny sea urchins left on the beach by the outgoing tide. Slipping through the heavy woods of pine and birch, he pretended to be Robin Hood in Sherwood Forest. Sometimes he stopped to explore the old cellar holes, traces of the families who lived there years ago. Bucky had counted eleven of these scattered on the island. Crossing the grassy meadow, he hunted for the wild strawberries that hugged the ground.

Life on an island-farm in 1906 was not just idleness and fun. Food had to be grown; supplies had to be brought in by boat. There were jobs enough for everyone, including eleven-year-old Bucky. Every day, rain or shine, he rowed to Eagle Island for the mail. In good weather Bucky never minded making that four-mile round trip. There were the dark blue waters to watch, seals to look for, the smell of salt and the fresh taste of Maine air to enjoy. He liked the exercise that made his shoulders broader and his muscles tough. But when he had to pull hard against the currents in thick fog, he wished there were an easier way to make the trip.

Leaving behind the mail in the Big House, Bucky headed back down to the pebbly beach. He hunted for pebbles to skip across the water. One, two, three, the stones skipped across, dipped touching the surface, skipped again, and finally sank. To be able to move so easily across the top of the water, and better yet, to see where he was going. . . . Still skimming stones, Bucky thought of all the living things that moved in the waters around his island. Codfish, lobsters, haddock, jellyfish—Maine waters were full of creatures large and small. He could see them all in his mind. It was then that the idea sneaked up on him. Excitement made the hairs on the back of his neck stand straight on end and his scalp prickled and itched. Yes, it could work. It *would* work.

With all the family gathered around the long table, dinner seemed to take forever that night. In the big stone fireplace, the flames climbed higher and took the chill from the long room. Grownups talked about the weather, the picnic plans for tomorrow. Voices bounced back from the low ceiling as the cousins argued over who should wind up the phonograph and which Victrola record should be played first after dinner. Bucky ignored them all. His attention was focused on the idea that had come to him earlier. At last the table was cleared. By the flickering light of the kerosene lamps, he set to work. The picture of the white jellyfish was clear in his head as he sketched, measured, and planned.

Nobody ever did chores faster than Bucky that next morning. With the firewood stacked neatly and fresh drinking water carried up from the spring, Bucky took off. He collected the tools and supplies on his way to the beach where the rowboat rested. There he hammered and nailed steadily, stopping just once to hunt for a big iron ring which he screwed into the stern of the rowboat. Then Bucky wiped his sweating hands on the sides of his knickers. Sliding the long pole through the ring, he was ready to push off. Only the sun and a single gull saw him pole out into the sparkling bay waters. But a crowd of children playing on the beach saw him when he came skimming back.

Cousin Andy shouted, "Hey, Bucky's back. Did you get the

mail *already?*" Then he frowned, shading his eyes against the sun with his hand. "What's that he's doing? Where are his oars?"

Splashing into the water with eager hands reaching out to pull the boat in, they were all talking excitedly. A grinning Bucky tried to answer all the questions at once.

"Yes," and he held up the mail as evidence. "Faster than rowing. Made it in half the time and you can see where you're going every minute."

"Let me see. Let *me* see."

To show them, Bucky lifted his long pole out of the water. At the end of it there was a weblike contraption, a folding cone something like an inside-out umbrella. When the pole slid down through the ring into the water, the cone or umbrella opened up to push against the water. It was like touching bottom. That hard shove from the rear sent the boat forward. As he pulled the pole back up and out of the water, the cone collapsed and became again an inside-out umbrella.

"Neat-o," said his younger brother, Wolcott. "But how do you steer?"

"Easy. When you put the pole in, put it in a little to the left of the stern and the boat goes left, a little to the right and the boat goes right."

Wolcott, who was only seven, hunted for words. "It's a . . . it's a push-pull pole."

"No," said Bucky. "It's a mechanical jellyfish." And he laughed out loud with the pure pleasure of what he had done this day.

Looking at Nature, he had taken one of her ways of moving creatures and put it to his own use. In years to come, he would look again and again to Nature's rules and ways; he would put them to work with surprising and successful results for all men.

The young boy, Bucky Fuller, knew two fixed points in the compass of his universe: Bear Island, Maine, and Milton, Massachusetts.

In the town of Milton, Columbine Avenue curves gently down into Central Avenue. Large wooded lots and big old houses give one the feeling of a country road. For years, people had come out from Boston to spend the summer in Milton. In the 1890's, more and more Bostonians decided it was a good place in which to live and raise a family the year round. Among these were Richard and Caroline Fuller, who drove out in their horse-drawn carriage to watch the building of their new house.

The house stood tall on a bluff with its entrance facing the side of the lot. It was a handsome house inside as well as out. The dining room was paneled with the white wood of the magnolia tree. White carved fireplaces warmed the dining room and living room. Dutch doors at the back of the hall and the den let cool breezes enter in the summer. A broad staircase with a cherry-wood banister led to the four bedrooms above and still higher to the servants' bedrooms in the attic. Richard Fuller's good friend and classmate, Henry Wadsworth Longfellow, Jr., had designed it for them. (Eleven years later he designed their Great House on Bear Island, too.)

July 12, 1895, was a rare summer day: clear, cloudless, and mildly warm. On that day, the new house saw the birth of a new member of the Fuller family. As the first son, he was doubly welcome and named Richard Buckminster for his father.

No one knew the strange world that the young Bucky lived in. Born both cross-eyed and far-sighted, he saw only blurs, blobs, and outlines. Looking back on his childhood, Bucky said, "While I saw two dark areas on human faces, I did not see a human eye or a teardrop or a human hair until I was four years old." He added, "There is luck in everything. My luck is that I was born cross-eyed." He was forced to use all his senses and brain power to understand the world around him. To recognize people, he depended on hearing their voices, touching them, and identifying the outline of their shapes. He never lost the habit of seeing things by wholes. Finding the large patterns in what he sees led him to important ideas and discoveries.

At four, Bucky was fitted with glasses. The heavy thick lenses made him look like a serious owlet. No more tumbling, no more stumbling over things he couldn't see. Those round, gold-rimmed glasses showed him the color of his big sister Leslie's eyes, baby brother Wooly's plump cheeks, his father's loving smile. And a million new things that he had only heard other people talking about: sparkling morning dew, brilliant butterflies, marching ants. He had heard the whispers of the wind through the trees. Now he saw with wonder and delight the veined green leaves that did the whispering. Everything looked newly made just for him. It marked the beginning of Bucky's lifelong love affair with the Universe.

Bucky's short, stocky legs pumped ever faster to explore the new world around him. The days were never long enough. Leslie, exercising the privilege of being the oldest, insisted that she should go to bed last. Bucky had a quick answer to that argument: *"Ladies first, gentlemen soon after."*

Bucky treasured most the time that he spent with his father. Mr. Fuller, a successful businessman, imported exotic teas and leathers. To find and buy these goods, he often took long trips to far parts of the globe. When Mr. Fuller was home, he and Bucky walked hand-in-hand on Sundays to St. Michael's Episcopal Church. On the way, his father would talk to him about God and the Fuller family. Bucky especially liked to hear the family stories.

Great-grandfather Timothy, a minister, had been a delegate from Massachusetts to the convention at which the Constitution was written. When the delegates did not put in a paragraph to forbid slavery, Timothy refused to sign the Constitution. Grandfather Arthur, also a minister, had not only made speeches against slavery but even fought in the Civil War. He was killed while leading a charge across the river at Freder-

Fullers in Milton, 1899: front, left to right, Cousin Richard, Wolcott, Leslie, Cousin Eugenia, Uncle Waldo Fuller; behind them, Bucky (left) and Cousin Duncan

icksburg. While other women kept themselves busy by raising a family, Great-aunt Margaret Fuller learned five languages and started a famous literary magazine, *The Dial*. No question about it. The Fullers were the kind of people who did more than just talk about their opinions and beliefs.

On weekdays, Bucky walked to school, a little one with a kindergarten and three grades. It was right next door to St. Michael's Church. Always exploring, always questioning, he played with the dried peas and sticks on the kindergarten table. He pushed sticks into the peas and discovered that a three-legged pyramid would stand upright. Adding on more and more triangles, his structure went out in different directions to become a curious tower. His teacher was impressed and called the other teacher to come admire the result.

Sixty years later, people crowded around to admire an airy, spidery creation in the garden of the Museum of Modern Art in New York City. Reworked with gold-colored aluminum tubes, the kindergarten tower of peas and sticks had turned into a soaring "Octet truss." It looked as if it should fall down. But, in fact, it could support enormous loads, a discovery important to the building industry.

Questions popped constantly into Bucky's mind, and sometimes he tried to find the answer himself. One afternoon his mother went out to have tea with her friends. Tiptoeing into her room, Bucky "borrowed" her diamond ring. Then, racing back to his room, he tested what he had heard. He dug the diamond hard against the windowpane, and the initials R.B.F. appeared. So it was true after all. Diamonds *could* cut glass. The satisfaction of finding out for himself was worth being sent upstairs without dinner. Besides, he had a talent for wheedling food out of the cook, so he didn't miss his dinner after all.

On many days, Bucky used his own special way to leave the house. From his bedroom window it was an easy jump down to the side porch roof. Dropping to the ground, he could cut through the woods to meet his best friend, Lincoln Pierce.

"Get up a game of Hare and Hounds?" he greeted Linc.

"Sure enough."

Patiently, the boys cut hundreds of pieces of paper to lay a trail.

"Both of *us* will be the Hare. You all be the Hounds," Bucky said to the others collected for the game.

The Hounds had to chase and catch them within an hour. On the west side of Milton was the Blue Hills Reservation, a state park. In the thick shrubs and endless trees of Blue Hills, the two boys could lay a trail and yet never get caught. It was no wonder that they got too confident.

Neither boy could resist the challenge of May Day; both were positive that they could hang a basket without being traced or caught.

"You know those girls can't run worth a darn," said Linc.

A wide grin spread across Bucky's face and he agreed. At the crack of dawn that May 1, two small figures hunted through the woods for spring flowers. They filled the May basket with pink cranesbills, white May apples, and violets. Making sure that no one was around to see them, they slipped up to Hathaway House, the dormitory for Milton Academy female students. After hanging the basket on the door, they raced off. Looking back, Linc saw with horror that Bucky had stopped.

"Run, Bucky, run!"

"I can't!" came Bucky's agonized cry. "I have to find my glasses. They fell off!"

Head down, Bucky was feeling through the grass. Linc turned back to help him. Behind them, a crowd of girls appeared with shrieks, shouts, and laughter. What a triumph it would be to catch those two little boys who teased the girls so. The red-faced, panting boys barely escaped. For consolation, they headed for Turner's Ice House at the pond. To snitch a piece of dripping ice to suck on was a better treat than money could buy.

Summertime days are supposed to be the laziest ones, but not Bucky's. The bustle and chores of packing for the yearly summer visit to Bear Island began early in the season. The one place where he could use all his mind and energy without

A family gathering at Bear Island, 1906: fourth from left, Grandma Andrews; in the center, Bucky (wearing glasses); tenth from left, Bucky's mother; at far right, Leslie and Wooly

getting into trouble was Bear Island. Exploring the island and the sea around it, Bucky found plenty to see and do.

He watched the fishermen deal with winds, currents, and ten-to fifteen-foot tides. Survival depended on their mastering Nature's rhythms. He noticed that they used Nature's own designs to do this. Trees bend in the wind, so boat masts were made of wood to bend but not break. A single strand of a spider's web is a fragile thing, but woven together, the strands have strength to catch and hold flies. The fishermen's woven nets did likewise, catching and holding fish. Bucky was learning some important lessons, with ships, sailors, and the sea as his teachers.

Nights on Bear Island, Bucky liked to stand outside and watch the stars. He thought of those stars, born millions of years ago, as a "live show of yesterdays." Feet braced wide apart, he faced the North Star. Fifteen, twenty, the minutes seemed endless. Then he had his reward. Yes, there was definitely a gentle pressure on his left foot. Everyone knows (with his mind) that the earth rotates. In Bucky's experiment, he could actually sense with his body the motion of the earth turning in the night sky.

Besides watching, Bucky learned by doing. His clever hands with long curving thumbs made good use of the island's rich resources. Using beach-dried driftwood, he whittled boats and all kinds of moving vehicles. The newest baby in the family, Rosamond, or Rosy, loved to play with those models. In *St. Nicholas Magazine*, he found the plans for a small cabin. He used lumber from the stands of good timber to build his first real structure. Although Bucky was just thirteen years old, he produced a solid building that any man would be proud to claim as his own. A snug little slope-roofed cabin, Birch Lodge is still used today to house visitors to the island.

Grandmother Andrews had bought one of the earliest gas-powered engines for the sloop. Making those early engines work was a tricky business. Breakdowns happened often and parts were scarce. Bucky used gallons of sweat and all his inventive ability to master that engine. In doing this, he learned to appreciate technology, which takes scientific ideas and puts them to work for practical purposes.

The main house on Bear Island

2   At the turn of the century, the world was exploding with new knowledge. Science and industry would bring more changes in the next twenty-five years than had occurred in the two hundred years before. Discoveries like Wilhelm Roentgen's x-rays and Marconi's wireless for sending messages were swiftly transformed into practical tools and machines. In 1895, the year of Bucky's birth, Charles Duryea produced the first American gas-engine car. Eight years later, three hundred cars were entered in a race from Paris to Bordeaux. Their average speed was 66 miles an hour.

Even in Milton, Bucky could see for himself some of these rapid changes. A Dr. Tudor received the very first automobile license given by the state of Massachusetts. By the time Bucky was ten years old, Americans had already spent $400 million on automobiles.

Meanwhile, the Wright Brothers managed to do the impossible. They actually put a machine heavier than air into flight at Kitty Hawk, North Carolina. Everyone's imagination was in the clouds now. A Count Zeppelin raised four thousand dollars to renew his experiments with aerial flight.

English, history, geography—the schoolbook lessons had not yet caught up with these events. Milton Academy, a private boarding school, drew students from all over New England. Bucky, like many who lived in Milton, attended the Academy as a day student. With Linc Pierce and a dozen others in the Sixth Form, Bucky wrestled with the same old questions: "At eight cents a foot, what will two yards of ribbon cost?" "Tell why Samuel Morse and Robert Fulton were famous men." Dutifully, Bucky filled his papers with answers.

Then without warning, the everyday routine and world of Bucky Fuller turned upside down. His father suffered a crippling stroke. No longer could he make trips to the Argentine and India to buy fine leathers and scented teas. Mr. Fuller became an invalid. The first stroke was followed by others, each leaving him more helpless than before. The family nursed him with love, but no one did more for him than Bucky.

"Who would have believed it of that young rascal Bucky?" asked Dr. Pierce, Linc's father. He shook his head in wonder. "Why, he sits for hours fanning Mr. Fuller. The way he leads his father by the hand and spends whole evenings reading aloud to him. . . . I've never seen a young boy show so much loving patience and care!"

While Dr. Pierce talked on about "compassion" and "pity," Bucky was choked with anger. Why couldn't medicine do something to *prevent* illnesses? Instead, the best that it could do was prescribe care afterward. It was like locking the barn door after the horse is gone. At the end of three long years, the strokes had stolen Mr. Fuller's mind and sight. On Bucky's fifteenth birthday in 1910, he first faced the pain of losing someone he loved, for Mr. Fuller died that day. One last time, Bucky, miserable and tear-stained, followed his father out of St. Michael's Church. This trip ended in Mt. Auburn Cemetery.

Now Mrs. Fuller found the family pocketbook much thinner. Money no longer came in from the importing business. But money went out constantly to feed four children, pay off medical bills, and keep up the house. An independent, strong-willed woman, she took the necessary steps to economize. The handyman who did the heavy chores was dismissed.

The very full load of a man's work around the house as well as the routine boy's chores rested on Bucky's shoulders now. Sifting the ashes was a dirty, unpleasant job but a necessary one. Clinkers, those unburned impurities, had to be thrown out. Half-burned coals left in the ash basket went back into the furnace to be thoroughly burned. Raking the driveway, carrying out the garbage—what an enormous amount of work it took to keep up that big wooden house that he called home! Strange how architects worked so hard to make every house look different. And yet the people inside those different-looking houses were all doing the same things: washing themselves, washing the clothes, cleaning out the dust. Why, almost every hour of each day in a house was spent cleaning up yesterday's dirt. "Why couldn't the *house* do the work?" was a simple question, but no one except Bucky asked such questions in 1911.

Work in school sometimes seemed almost as exasperating as his chores at home. In geometry class, the teacher drew points and lines on the blackboard and said they were imaginary. Two parallel lines made a plane and that didn't exist either. Then she stacked the planes one on top of the other to make a cube and *that did* exist, she said. It seemed unreasonable to Bucky. His hand shot up in the air.

"Please, I have some questions. If that cube exists, how much does it weigh? What is its temperature? How long has it been there?"

There were no answers.

"Don't try to be funny, Richard Fuller. You are impertinent!" the teacher snapped.

Bucky Fuller's love of mathematics had tripped him up. He had forgotten the rules of the game. Rules in those days

Milton Academy in 1913

Bucky in Milton, 1911

said that adults know all the answers; children are supposed to keep their mouths shut and listen. He shrugged his shoulders, reminding himself to keep questions and doubts to himself. Years later he found the answers to this unsatisfactory geometry of imaginary lines and planes by discovering his *own* geometry of forces.

No matter if Bucky got put down. With his mind and spirit, he always came back up like a yo-yo. His science teacher, Homer Le Sourd, encouraged students to explore and experiment. A special section newly glued into the back of the physics book gave them facts about the expanding field of electricity. And Milton Academy had a laboratory complete with electric motor power to drive the tools for working with metal and wood. Few schools in the country were so well equipped. Like many boys, Bucky must have made at least twenty triplanes that he sent gliding out the attic window. Like many adults, Mrs. Fuller saw it all as nonsense. Her voice would float up to the attic: "Bucky, enough of playing games. Stop wasting your time. Get back to work!"

One adult at least continued to play games with these foolish airplanes. W. Starling Burgess, a Milton graduate, came back to school to deliver a lecture. In 1910, Burgess had made the first airplane flight in New England, going almost ten miles from Plum Island in Massachusetts to Ipswich, Massachusetts. Eagerly, the boys watched the lantern slides that showed Burgess's experiments on Plum Island. Bucky hardly dreamed then that one day Burgess would be working for R. Buckminster Fuller to engineer a new kind of transport.

Bucky did very well indeed in any field that he cared about. With ferocious energy and enthusiasm, he tried out for the football team and won the desired spot of quarterback. He also won the respect of his classmates, particularly since they knew he couldn't see much on the field without his glasses.

"How do you do it, Bucky? How can you tell who is who and where to pass?"

"Shapes. Outlines, patterns." Bucky shrugged.

Because Bucky hated being "different," he suffered every time he went out on the field to play. All the other boys wore regulation leather helmets. Bucky wore a cheap, funny-looking thing that his mother had bought. A helmet was a helmet to Mrs. Fuller and she could not understand Bucky's desperate wish to have the same helmet as everyone else.

Shoulders squared out from hours of rowing, his stocky figure looked even shorter on the ball field. Opponents from St. Mark's and Groton who came to play might smile at the sight of him. By the end of the play, they looked at him with new respect.

"It's like trying to tackle a greased keg shooting over Niagara Falls."

In the classroom, Bucky used his energy to master the Latin verbs which he hated and to sing for the Glee Club with gusto.

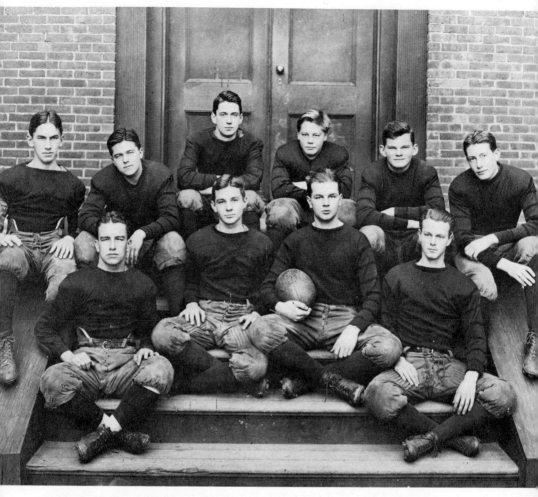

Milton Academy football team, 1911; Bucky is first on the left in the front row

School records show that he got passing grades in Classics and Latin but earned honors in science and mathematics.

When Bucky graduated from Milton Academy in 1913, there was no question about what he would do next. With all the family helping, Mrs. Fuller scraped together enough money for Bucky's college tuition and board. There was no money for extras, but Richard Buckminster Fuller would enter Harvard University as so many Fullers had before him.

3 "What a jolly thing life is!" said the handsome college man in the *McClure's Magazine* ad. And that is exactly how Bucky felt as he entered Harvard. Over the years, he had built in his mind a romantic picture of life at Harvard. Now he felt a shiver of delight at being a part of this imagined world of superathletes and godlike heroes.

A red brick wall skirted the edges of the Harvard Yard. Within the wall, there were tall elm trees, green grass, and stillness. He seemed to be miles away from the bustle, noise, and dirt of the city of Boston. Crossing the Yard, he could hear chapel bells ringing, young voices calling. The Yard was a dream come true, and Bucky moved into his single room with a sense of adventure and high hopes.

One of these hopes was to win a place on the Harvard football team. After all, Milton quarterbacks before him had made the Harvard team. During the tryouts, he threw himself against the line of defense with explosive energy. Cr-rack! He came out of the tryouts with one broken kneecap and one less hope.

Now cold winds whipped the leaves from the trees in the Yard. As he went to classes, Bucky hardly felt these hints of winter. It was the classes themselves that he began to dread. Musical composition, German literature, art appreciation— working on those subjects was sheer drudgery. Why hadn't he chosen the math and science that he loved so much? Those subjects had been more like games than serious studies. Perhaps he had thought college should be a place to explore more "difficult" subjects. What a mistake. The courses became like those miserable chores around the house. They were a necessary evil by which he "earned the right to live in the Harvard community."

Worse yet was the discovery that he made about life outside the classroom. In those days, the social clubs at Harvard ran everything. Although he had heard about the clubs all his life, he had never dreamed of the effect they had. All people were not equal in this undemocratic system. The clubs measured a

Bucky at about the time he went to Harvard

man by who his father was and how much money he had. Only a select few were invited to join. Some (but not all) of the captains and heroes of the athletic field were chosen as well. Everyone else was locked out of the fun and many of the pleasures of social life.

One by one, old Milton friends were asked into that special closed system. But Bucky had no father, no money, and none of the smooth charm and glamour of a football hero. He was very simply an odd-looking, poor boy, shorter than almost anyone, with thick owl lenses and a stubbornly independent way of thinking. By January, Bucky faced the unhappy truth. No club would choose him. He felt doubly disgraced. His high hopes of making the team and of exciting new friendships had been crushed. Even the pleasure and excitement of learning were missing. He spent dreary days studying for exams in subjects that he disliked. It was a lonely and depressed Bucky who walked across the Harvard Yard. By the gray light of winter's days, the bare Yard with its wall looked more like a prison to him now.

So what if he passed his midyear exams? Nothing would change. Why should he sit there looking forward to three more years of the same loneliness and hurt? For Bucky, to think was to do. Moving fast, he packed his bags and went out the door. There was more than one way to have fun and more than one place to have it in. After a visit to the bank, he raced for the train.

"Runaway, runaway, runaway." The words fit the rhythm of the clacking train wheels. Every cent of the money that was supposed to pay his bills for the year at Harvard was in his pocket. Grand and glorious New York City was ahead of him and he meant to make the most of it.

First he signed in at one of the best hotels in New York, then he bought a ticket to the most popular show on Broadway, the *Follies*. One beautiful girl after another appeared in gorgeous costume. How he would love to meet these glamorous creatures! And why couldn't he do that, too? At this moment nothing seemed impossible. With a grand flourish, he ordered dozens of red roses and bottles of champagne sent with his card to the dancers. By the next night, he felt bold enough to present himself at the backstage door. Marilyn Miller, the stunning blonde star, welcomed this young fan. Still playing the role of a sophisticated rich man, Bucky invited *all* the girls to dinner at one of New York's most elegant restaurants.

At the table there was warmth, gaiety, and laughter. What a pity those snobby classmates weren't there to see him. He, the rejected Bucky Fuller, had captured the attention and company of Broadway's most beautiful girls. He refused for now to think about the end of his spree. It was enough to be with people who appreciated his generosity, laughed at his jokes, and clapped their hands at the funny verses he made up on the spot.

When his money came to an end, Bucky boarded the train back to Harvard. For over a week he had skipped his classes and completely missed taking his exams. While Harvard couldn't "fire" him for spending his own money, they could and did dismiss him for "irresponsible conduct." Squaring his shoulders, Bucky returned to Milton to face his family. He carried the double disgrace of having squandered his money and of being the first one in five generations of Fullers to flunk out of Harvard.

"Bucky, Bucky, you have no respect for money. You *must* mend your ways or they'll lead you straight to the penitentiary!" Seriously worried, Mrs. Fuller called a conference of family members to decide what to do with her black sheep. One of the uncles voiced his blunt opinion. Bucky needed to learn how much hard work went into earning a dollar. Then he would appreciate the values of a college education. Ship him up to Canada to their cousin's cotton mill, the uncle suggested. All agreed. The ideal solution. To be sent far away from family and friends, to work hard with his hands seemed a just punishment. He could come back when he showed he had learned his lesson.

Once again, Richard Buckminster Fuller found himself riding on a train. What a difference, though, between New York City and the end of this trip. He got off the train at Sherbrooke, a small manufacturing town in the Province of Quebec. Reporting for work, he saw a bare new mill building in a bare, bleak countryside. Huge crates, little crates, masses of parts and tools were waiting to be put together. It was a strange new

world of shop foremen and machinists, of hammering and bang-
ing. Despite the noise and confusion, Bucky felt his spirits start
to rise. He liked men and he liked machines. Here there were no
special patterns of social power. Each man was appreciated for
the work that he did. Bucky threw himself into the work with
his own special passion and eagerness.

All of the machinery and parts came from England and
France. Some of these arrived damaged and broken. Soon,
Bucky's special task became that of finding new parts or repairing the broken ones. He studied the metals, their weights, and
how they performed under different conditions. By necessity,
he had to retrace the original steps leading to the invention of
these parts. Making many different kinds of small things, he was
forced into thinking about how to bring together whole sets of
different parts.

"Bucky, I believe this part is actually better than the original one sent to us," said the chief engineer. "You're a good
designer. For your own sake and knowledge, you should keep a
sketchbook of your work."

Flushed with happiness, Bucky followed his advice. The
sketchbook, the experiments with tools and metals, made a kind
of mental bank account from which he drew all his life.

Mrs. Fuller read his letters carefully, and read too the letters
from the bosses. All the reports said that he was "a good and
able boy," from which she concluded hopefully that Bucky
had changed his ways. Harvard University agreed. He could
become a member of the class entering in 1914.

After a summer on beloved Bear Island, Bucky settled once
again into a single room at Harvard. The other freshmen were
all younger than he. Neither the classes nor the social system
had changed. After working in the real world, both seemed even
more unreal and ridiculous than before. How could his good
intentions hold against this setup? This semester was, in fact,
worse than the first one. In flat despair, Bucky behaved exactly
the same way he did the first time. He stayed away from
classes and spent all his money on foolish "larks." Once again,

Bucky at Bear Island

Harvard University expelled him for "lack of interest." Grown-ups in the family and friends shook their heads. "Bucky has a genius," they said. "A genius for getting into trouble!"

His independence and energy seemed to lead him only to bad endings. Perhaps his mother was right, perhaps he would end up in the penitentiary. Bucky recognized that he had caused his family pain and shame. But, at the same time, he felt an enormous sense of relief. He was free at last from the dreadful social system at Harvard. He was free, in fact, to go about the business of real learning.

Hunting for a job in New York City, he found one with Armour and Company, a meat-packing house. It was a revelation to see all the work that went into getting meat to the dinner table. Pork shot down chutes to the cellar for curing; beef was cut into quarters and moved into the chilly cooler room. Finally, the quarters of beef were carried on men's backs to the trucks. "Heave," the foremen shouted in icy puffs of breath. Bucky gave silent thanks for the summers on Bear Island. They had given him a tough, strong frame and the good balance he needed to lug the heavy sides of beef. Work for Bucky started at three o'clock in the morning. He moved about the still sleeping city, loading and unloading trucks in the lighted islands of the markets, filling the huge holds of waiting ships at the docks. With luck, he finished work at five in the afternoon. Fourteen hours of hard, dirty work every day. Bucky did the work well and even enjoyed it.

In his report, the branch manager noted that this was a bright, hard-working young man and the company should be thinking of moving him up the ladder. The decision was made that he should be given experience in all parts of the business. So Bucky moved from branch to branch around New York City and New Jersey. That first job in Canada had taught him about the making of goods. This one showed him the pattern and systems for moving the goods to men. Solving the knotty problems of getting more meat to greater numbers of people gave him satisfaction. "Turnover and turnabout" were the key words to this business, he realized as he mapped out loading and unloading schedules.

In that summer of 1915, his sister Leslie and her husband, Edward P. Larned, had rented a house on Long Island. When they invited him out for a weekend, Bucky accepted quickly. Besides the chance to escape the city's summer heat, it gave him time to spend at the ocean that he loved so much. He met old friends and made new ones during his visit.

One of these old friends invited him to a dance.

"Come along, Bucky. There are some pretty girls here you ought to meet."

The young girls in their ankle-length thin summer dresses looked like bright butterflies. Bucky grinned. Already his foot was keeping time to the music. When it came to meeting pretty girls and dancing, he was more than ready.

Anne Hewlett. That name belonged to a slim girl. She had laughing dark eyes and a cloud of soft dark hair. And then there was her sister Anglesea, better known as Anx. The younger girl had the same smooth complexion but blonde curling hair and blue eyes. Bucky was impressed by these pretty sisters. The next day he went happily and eagerly with his friend to call at the Hewlett house.

Much as Bucky enjoyed his work, his thoughts strayed

elsewhere now—to the sloops waiting to be sailed on the week-end, the beach picnics with driftwood fires and young people strumming banjos and singing, and especially to those pretty Hewlett girls.

As the summer drew to a close, the summer cottages were closed up one by one. Families packed their bags and moved back to the city. Glumly, Bucky set off on that last weekend to say good-by to the Hewletts. When Anne invited him to dinner in their Brooklyn home, his spirits skyrocketed. Contrary to that old proverb, all good things did not have to come to an end.

Anne was the oldest of ten children and Bucky was the first young man she had invited into the family circle. Looking around the Hewletts' dining room table, Bucky was not so sure that he was a lucky fellow after all. To have twelve pairs of eyes turned with interest on his every movement was unnerving. Fortunately, Mr. Hewlett was a gentle man who kept the lively young Hewletts from making too many comments about the newcomer.

Soon Bucky became a regular caller at the house in Brooklyn. "Anne has a boyfriend . . . Anne has a boyfriend . . . ," the younger Hewletts chanted loudly and made sure that the young couple never had a moment of privacy. Sometimes they escaped for a quiet moment by joining Mrs. Hewlett, a semi-invalid, in her upstairs bed-sitting room. Only a truly determined young man would have continued this courtship. Bucky was quite certain now in his own mind and heart that Anne was the girl with whom he wanted to share his life. His jokes, comic verses, and love of fun soon won over the noisy, teasing young ones in her family. They declared him an honorary Hewlett. More important, Anne showed encouraging signs of returning his feelings.

Not everyone in her family felt so kindly toward him as a suitor. One of her grandfathers in particular objected. After all, Bucky was a poor boy with bad eyesight who had been thrown out of college twice. He had no profession and earned only a tiny salary. What could he offer a wife? Bucky worried about that, too. But, being Bucky, he went right on spending large amounts of that tiny salary on huge bouquets of red roses for Anne.

During a trip across the country, Anne finally made up her mind. When she returned, she accepted Bucky's proposal. Following the custom of the times, Bucky promptly applied to Mr. Hewlett for his daughter's hand in marriage. The Hewletts, who had grown fond of Bucky, consented and the engagement was announced in the summer of 1916. Bucky worked harder than ever and for the first time in his life tried to save money for the future.

Anne Hewlett, at about the time she became engaged to Bucky

4 For young and old, the future seemed clouded with doubt and uncertainty. People everywhere— Germans, Frenchmen, Englishmen, Turks, Russians— were being swept up into armies or were fleeing from armies as their countries declared war against one another.

In this first world-wide war, the fighting spread to every continent except the Americas and to every ocean except those surrounding the Poles. Every day, newspaper headlines grew larger and blacker with horror stories, U-boat sinkings, and casualty lists. How could America stay out of the war? When Germany began sinking American ships, there was no longer any hope of peace for the United States. President Wilson broke off relations with Germany and young men everywhere hurried to enlist in the armed forces.

With his experience in boats, Bucky clearly would be most useful in the Navy. With his eye problems, however, there was no way that he could pass the physical examination. Bucky refused to give up hope. Wasn't the Navy looking desperately for small boats to patrol the coast? And didn't the Fullers own such a small boat, the *Wego*? At last Bucky had a scheme, but first he had to convince his mother and then persuade the Navy. His scheme worked. When Mrs. Fuller offered the *Wego* for patrol duty, the Navy accepted both the boat and Bucky as its commander.

"Chief Boatswain Fuller." It was a title to be proud of, the highest rank a noncommissioned officer could hold. Best of all, he could pick his own crew. Linc Pierce had already agreed to be first mate and his brother Wolcott, too, was keen to join them.

Up at Bear Island, Bucky worked furiously to prepare the *Wego* for active duty. Late in February 1917, the *Wego* became a Navy Scout Patrol boat officially assigned to guard the Maine coast. Only one problem remained to be licked: He missed Anne badly. Since a chief boatswain's pay was more than twice what he had earned at Armour, there was no reason now why he

The crew of the U.S.S. Wego, Bar Harbor, Maine, 1917; Bucky is at the helm, third from right

could not support a wife. A proud and happy Bucky sat down to write to Anne.

Anne's letter discussed the practical details and preparations: Grandmother planned to use larkspur and hollyhocks to decorate the house; Anx, of course, would be in the wedding party. Most important, she urged him to be sure to have leave for that whole weekend.

Important events in Bucky's life had a way of happening on his birthday. Certainly one of the happiest events was his marriage to Anne Hewlett on his twenty-second birthday, July 12, 1917. The wedding took place at Grandmother Hewlett's

summer place. Built in 1730, Rock Hall was one of the most historic old mansions on Long Island. Young officers in Washington's army had visited and danced there. Now, more than a
century later, the Hall was filled again with young men in
uniform.

On the flag-hung, flower-decorated porch, Bucky stood with
Linc Pierce who was the best man. Both looked stiff but splendid
in their Navy dress uniforms. A harp played softly. As the
great-grandfather clock in the main hall chimed five, the violins
and cello began the wedding march. The side door of the ve-
randa opened and Anne stepped into view. In a simple white or-
gandy dress with a flounced skirt, she seemed a vision from the
past. Looking more solemn and owllike than ever, Bucky took
a deep breath and stepped forward.

After the ceremony, laughter and cheers greeted the toasts
to the newlyweds. Anne had young Rosy help to cut the cake
with the long shining sword that was a tradition in military
weddings. The musicians serenaded them with the strains of
"Oats, peas, beans, and barley grow. . . ." Passing under the arch
of swords and ducking the showers of confetti, the couple ran
down the steps to the waiting motorcar.

Almost immediately, Bucky had to report back for duty.
He was moved up to command a larger boat, the *Inca*, and sent
to Virginia where the Navy had a new school for training pilots.
Sometimes the seaplanes coming in for a landing "porpoised,"
that is, they came in too steeply and tripped over their own
pontoons, sending the nose of the plane down into the water. As
a crash boat, the *Inca* had the job of rescuing these men. It was
an important job, but a heartbreaking one, too, as Bucky soon
found out. When the plane capsized completely, the stunned,
belted-in pilot hung upside down in the water. Often the trapped
pilot drowned before swimmers from the *Inca* could reach or
free him.

These tragedies haunted Bucky. More, they filled him with
the same sick anger that he had felt at his father's illness. There

must be a way. There *must* be a way to prevent this from happening. Science and technology put wings on men. Science and technology should be able to save them. Muttering and scribbling, Bucky worried over the problem every spare moment. He made countless sketches until at last the familiar current of discovery shot through him.

"I know it will work," said Bucky to the station commander. He looked more confident than he felt. The two men bent over the working drawings. The mast was to be placed in the stern. The boom would have to be reinforced, of course. The grappling hook and winch could then tip the whole plane right side up immediately.

"I like the looks of your life-saving hook. We'll give it a try,

Anne and Bucky's wedding party, July 12, 1917

Fuller," the commander decided. He gave orders to have a model built on the *Inca*.

In practicing on already wrecked seaplanes, the device seemed to work. It hoisted the planes right out of the water easily enough. But would it be speedy enough to save men's lives? Watching the sky, Bucky knew when the testing day came. He could sense that this particular plane was coming in at too steep an angle. He shouted orders to move his men and ship. Within minutes the *Inca* was at the side of the capsized plane. Now the plane was up. Dozens of hands fumbled to free the dangling pilot. Then the body was down on the deck. The doctor's hands worked steadily to pump water out of the lungs. Stretching, stretching, the minutes dragged on. The eyelids fluttered, opened, and the young pilot began to vomit! Bucky Fuller grinned as the crew cheered wildly.

That wide grin stretched even farther across his face some days later. Standing at attention, Bucky listened to Commander Bellinger. America needed more officers and needed them quickly. So the Navy had created a special program for training its brightest and most able young men to become officers. Despite the fact that Bucky had no college degree, the commander was recommending him for special appointment to the program.

At the Naval Academy in Annapolis, Maryland, Bucky plunged into the hardest, most challenging work he had met to date. Unlike the work at Harvard, the classroom lessons here were tied directly to practical questions. How do ships survive the forces at sea? Force exists in the form of waves and winds. Its pull is a line whose effect can be plotted and measured. These lines which describe actual physical events are called vectors. Richard Buckminster Fuller found that he much preferred this geometry of vectors to that of his schoolboy days with its nonexistent points and lines.

Bucky's thoughts were ranging far beyond the lessons of both his textbooks and seamanship. He felt a new confidence as he stood on the deck. Looking back at the wake of the ship, he saw millions of white bubbles. He began wondering idly how many millions of bubbles were there in the wake. Bubbles are spheres, of course, and he knew that to measure a sphere you used the famous mathematical symbol of pi. But pi is an irrational number, one that is a never-ending, nonrepeating decimal. It struck him that in chemistry all the elements combine in beautiful whole numbers, never frustrating fractions. At what point did Nature round off the decimal in making those millions of bubbles?

No, Bucky decided suddenly, Nature did not use pi in her spheres, whether they were bubbles in the water or elsewhere. Nature must be using a different system of arithmetic and geometry and it must be a real beauty. It seemed to him that her system must be the same in all her models and creations. After all, it was man who had set up separate departments of chemistry and physics, not Nature. He felt convinced that by charting and observing Nature over a long enough period of time, he could find that single system. And he was even more convinced that it would turn out to be a very, very simple one. His decision that day to find Nature's own geometry was to lead him on a fifty-year hunt.

Engineering, ballistics, mathematics—the Navy was cramming three years of work into that three-month course at Annapolis. Bucky enjoyed every minute of it. After the disasters at Harvard, he found great satisfaction in knowing that he could handle the toughest kind of class work. His grades and rank in class proved his ability once and for all. As in those summers at Bear Island, he had enough here to take up his extraordinary energy.

All the cadets, whether married or single, had to live in the barracks, but Bucky was luckier than the others. By chance, his brother-in-law's family owned two hotels in Annapolis. So without spending too much money, Anne could stay near him. After evening parade, they would meet and walk slowly back to her hotel. It was like frosting on the cake to have Anne's company at the end of the day. Words would spill out of him eagerly as he shared some of the new ideas and thoughts bombarding him every day.

Bucky's mind, which always looked for patterns, had noted a difference in the Navy's education of its officers. While at Harvard everybody talked about specializing, the Navy gave its brightest students a general course, one that gave them a picture of the whole system. In his writings later, Bucky concluded that the Navy had the right idea. To solve the problems of life in the twentieth century, man needed the broadest possible education. He pointed out: "We're the only living creatures meant to be 'generalists.' We're the only ones who can live and travel on land, on the water, and in the air. If Nature intended Man to be a specialist, she would have made him so. She would have him born with one eye and a microscope attached to it."

Although it was a time of war and anxiety, it was also a time of love and contentment for the young Fullers. In those months at Annapolis, Bucky enjoyed the pleasure of learning, the satisfaction of accomplishment, and the added joy of having his beloved Anne at his side.

Graduation brought the rank of ensign and a new assignment. He served now as a communications officer and personal aide to Admiral Gleaves. Because the admiral was in charge of the secret information on convoys, Bucky kept track of the movements and location of every single ship at sea. Using codes to communicate with the ships, he had to send enormous amounts of information with as few words as possible. Bucky knew that a captain who misunderstood him might take a wrong action with fatal results for his ship and men. Appreciating the importance of his words, Bucky adopted a rule that he has kept all his life: A message must be absolutely clear. One other of Bucky's duties helped him polish his skill with words still further. He edited the *Transport*, a newspaper published for the men at sea.

Bucky working as aide to Admiral Gleaves

5   To send the glad news on November 11, 1918, Bucky needed only two words: "War's over!" On land, bells clanged; at sea, ships' whistles blew. People everywhere danced in the streets, hugged and kissed one another in joyous relief. The signing of the Armistice signaled the end of the war. It meant also that the work of building peace had to begin. When President Wilson announced his plan to sail for Europe, the news had a special importance for Bucky Fuller. His latest assignment was to the *George Washington*, the very ship chosen to carry the President to Europe.

Workers swarmed over the ship repairing, repainting, and redecorating it. Stepping over the boards and around the buckets, Bucky made his way to the gangplank to greet the man coming aboard. Dr. Lee DeForest, who had invented a new kind of radio tube in 1907, had come to oversee the installation of special radio equipment. The two men greeted one another as old friends. Earlier, DeForest had carried out his experiments in radio telephony on a small ship that Bucky commanded. The inventor had devised a radio set so light yet powerful that it could be used in an airplane to communicate with land and sea.

The pioneers of the West had disappeared, but Bucky had the chance to work with a pioneer on the frontier of technology. The system being installed on the *George Washington* would be the first successful attempt to carry voices beyond seventy miles. Men miles apart could talk both instantly and *wireless-ly*. Drawing on his experiences, Bucky once again saw a larger pattern. In the notebook which he kept, he observed that the world was moving "from the *track* [of trains and trolleys] to the *trackless* [to trucks and airplanes for moving goods and men]." "We're going from the wire to the wireless, the visible to the invisible." True progress, he concluded, means "doing more with less."

While Bucky was on active duty, Anne had moved back to live with her family. She, too, had important news for Bucky. On December 12, 1918, a tiny, fragile baby girl, Alexandra Willets Fuller, was born. Hurrying ashore for that event, Bucky looked into the cradle with awe and delight. What an extraordinary privilege it was to be given this gift of new life! And what a marvel of design!

Anne Fuller needed all the help and support that her family could give her that winter of 1919. The great, killing influenza epidemic which had begun the year before continued to sweep through the United States. Alexandra caught it and struggled to survive. With loving care and around-the-clock nursing, she pulled through. Before they could rejoice, the Fullers were stunned by new disaster. Alexandra fell ill with spinal meningitis, an almost always fatal disease. Miraculously, she survived that, too, only to be stricken later with infantile paralysis. How much can the human body endure, parents and doctors wondered helplessly. The baby more or less overcame this last attack. There were traces of paralysis left, but Bucky and Anne were grateful to have her alive.

Bucky knew a vital decision must be made. From the day he entered the Navy, Bucky had felt at home. The sea and ships had been his earliest teachers and love. He wanted to remain in the Navy. But in the Navy, a man cannot pick and choose his assignments. He must go wherever he is sent. It might be a tropical, mosquito-infested base or a barren, cold, storm-swept station. How could Alexandra survive such conditions? Her fragile, match-thin body still needed constant care and nursing. Much as he loved the Navy, he loved his infant daughter more. Lieutenant (j.g.) Richard Buckminster Fuller transferred to inactive or reserve status on August 28, 1919, and returned to work for Armour and Company.

Despite the pain-filled days, there were intervals when Alexandra was better. Then Bucky's optimism and high spirits took over. Packing up, the whole family caught the night boat to Boston to attend Linc Pierce's wedding on June 30, 1920. Fog delayed the boat so that they scooted up the aisle of the Unitarian Church after the service had begun. Too late for Bucky to play his part as an usher but in plenty of time to congratulate Linc and kiss his pretty bride, Ada. Greeting old friends at the reception, the Fullers put aside their worries and cares for the moment.

It would seem as if Bucky should no longer have any money worries. His job at Armour now paid him fifty dollars a week, a very good salary for that time. But nurses and medicines used up almost all of the money. In 1922, when an old Navy friend offered a new job with more pay in a company manufacturing trucks, Bucky took it gladly. He tackled the job of national sales manager for Kelly-Springfield Truck Company with his usual ferocious energy. New business rolled in steadily for three months. In the middle of his success, he heard the unbelievable news. The owners of the company, which also made tires, had decided to close down the truck-making part of the company. Dismissed! Out of a job almost before he had begun. How could a man have confidence in himself and his efforts? How was he to meet the expenses of his family?

Fortunately, Bucky still had his position as a reserve officer in the Navy. He returned to active duty on a ship that was being used for summer training of men.

A depressed Bucky stepped on board the *Eagle Boat 15*. The feeling of a deck under his feet again brought a small smile to the corners of his mouth. He saw sailors saluting smartly and hurrying to carry out commands. The small smile widened into his typical toothy grin. It was impossible to continue feeling depressed when he was once again on board a ship. Once more —as always in the Navy, at least—Fuller's luck held up, for the commander of the squadron took an instant liking to him. Vincent Astor was as tall and thin as Bucky was short and stocky, but the two young men shared the same love for ships and flying. In fact, Vincent Astor was a multimillionaire who owned his own seaplane, a five-seater. This "flying boat," as it was called, had all the latest technical discoveries and improvements. Usually a full-time pilot was at the controls, but often Astor let Bucky take a turn as copilot. In the pleasure of piloting that plane, Bucky could forget momentarily his joblessness and debts.

When the summer training program ended, the friendship between the two men continued. Astor, who was leaving on business for Europe, proposed to Bucky that he continue using the seaplane. After all, the plane would just be sitting in the hangar while Astor was gone. Everything—fuel, hangar space, pilot—was paid for through the end of October. He concluded by saying, "The more you fly it, the better."

Who could resist such an opportunity? Who would want to resist? With wholehearted enthusiasm, Bucky took up the offer. Since planes were still a novelty that made news, the newspapers reported these flights solemnly, talking about the value of seaplanes in coast defense and scout work.

Meanwhile, Bucky and Anne planned a vacation for the middle of September. No chug-chugging on dusty roads for the Fullers; they would take their vacation like birds—in the air. If Bucky thought Anne might be nervous about flying, there was no clue or sign of it on her face. Gazing out the windows which were set at the passenger's elbow height, she looked as calm and comfortable as a lady going for a drive in her limousine.

Tilting in great circles, the plane began to climb into the sky. Through smoky wisps of clouds, they could see the land below in rifts and patches. They put down at Newport, Rhode Island, for lunch and paid a call on Admiral Gleaves, Bucky's old wartime commander. By dinnertime they were in Wiscasset, Maine, and visiting with Bucky's mother. On Thursday they flew up to Bear Island, where they had three glorious days of crisp, clear Maine air and the golden sunshine of Indian summer.

Bucky made countless short hops each day around Penobscot Bay. Jim Hardie, caretaker of the island, did not trust this strange air-sea machine. When he went up with Bucky, Hardie carried an oar with him. Whatever might happen, he at least was prepared to paddle. A shrewd fisherman, he did more than marvel at the clear view of the bottoms of the shoals and reefs. He spotted new sites to put lobster pots and dredge for scallops. Everywhere the flying boat landed, it was a magnet drawing

A New York Herald *photograph shows Bucky flying Vincent Astor's seaplane on the 1922 vacation trip*

hundreds of curious sightseers, summer visitors, and native fishermen.

Leaving Bear Island on Monday, the Fullers took to the air again. They began their leisurely return trip, making stops at Bar Harbor and Boston. Skimming over the top of the surf, the plane climbed up to ride over Great Head and Schooner Head, the highest bluffs on the Atlantic coast. Bucky charted his speed. The plane did 120 miles an hour with no difficulty at all. Cutting the motor, he let the plane glide in silence for a moment. A wave of his hand called Anne's attention to the panoramic view framed in the window. Below, the waters lapping an island were tinted red by the sun's rays. They were gliding over Isle au Haut where Nathaniel Bowditch wrote his book, *The New American Practical Navigator*, the sailor's bible for navigating the seas.

While the seas had been mapped and charted, man sailed now in a new ocean, an unbroken air ocean with land as the bottom. For traveling through the air over our curving earth, he needed a new kind of geography. The old flat maps would never do; there was too much distortion as you moved away from the equator. Someone would have to map new routes through this air ocean.

Riding high in the sky, Fuller could see the need but did not realize then that he would be the one to fill it. A sudden bump of air brought him back to the needs of the moment. With the motors switched on and wind at their back, they were reaching their highest speed yet—130 miles an hour. Gliding down to the hangar at Port Washington, Bucky gave a satisfied sigh. They had covered seventeen hundred miles all told without a single hitch or repair needed.

It was to be the last satisfied moment the Fullers had that fall. Cold November winds blew new illness into their household and a chill into their hearts. Alexandra came down with pneumonia. Could they dare to hope that she might overcome this as she had so many other ailments? But her frail body could stand no more. Her lungs clogged by bronchial pneumonia, she died on November 14, 1922, just before her fifth birthday.

Her death threw Bucky into a deep depression from which he could not seem to pull out. He felt a crazy sense of personal guilt for her death and was convinced that it need not have happened. Raging against her fate, he felt that there should have been a way to prevent it. If the world had adequate shelters, houses that weren't drafty and overcrowded. . . . Our environment is really a hodgepodge of ignorance, he concluded.

For the first time in his life, Bucky could not bounce back. In that dark, gloomy autumn, he seemed to have lost everything: his daughter, his job, his zest for living. It was his father-in-law, J. Monroe Hewlett, who opened a new window of interest for Bucky. An architect as well as a painter, Mr. Hewlett had been tinkering with a new kind of building block. He asked Bucky to look at the result. The big block looked something like a giant shredded-wheat biscuit, the kind people eat for breakfast. Mr. Hewlett had taken loose straw, soaked it with cement, and molded it into a block.

Explaining the advantages of his "brick" in construction, Mr. Hewlett pointed out that it was almost impossible to break or crack it. It was tough but light, weighing just two pounds. Stacked up, such blocks could serve as molds for building a concrete-framed wall. Another advantage lay in the two holes at each end of the block. If you lined the blocks up and poured concrete down the holes, you gave the concrete frame added strength and support. Used in this way, the blocks also acted as insulators against cold and moisture.

Bucky thought it was an extremely clever, good design. Mr. Hewlett, who had great respect for Bucky's creative ability and talents, was encouraged by his interest. Hewlett had one last question. Would Bucky be willing to work on translating the brick idea into a whole system of construction? Some way had to be found to produce the bricks in quantity. Factory location would be important—it should be near good transportation for distributing the bricks. Patents had to be applied for. Hewlett's faith in Bucky's ability to solve the problems restored Bucky's own confidence. With respect and love, the two men shook hands firmly on the deal and the Stockade Building System company was born.

As president of the company, Bucky had more than enough work to fill the days now. He set about inventing machinery to mold the bricks in quantity. Drawing upon his business experience with Armour, he worked out costs and ways to sell the bricks. He used his experiences in the Canadian factory to lay out the machinery in his new factory. What he didn't know about the building industry itself, he pushed himself to learn.

What he learned about the "shelter tailors" of our world caused him to shake his head in amazement. The business of building seemed to be stuck somewhere in the Dark Ages. Certainly he found it to be the slowest industry in the world to accept new ideas (Portland cement had been known and available for forty-two years before anyone dared to use it in buildings). Despite the slowness of the industry and unions to accept new ideas, some customers decided they wanted the Stockade Build-

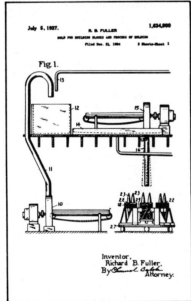

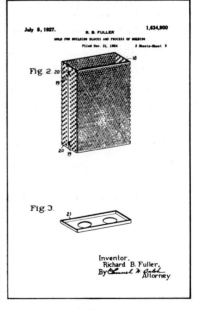

Above: a garage wall made of Stockade Blocks; below: two drawings from the Stockade Block manufacturing patent

ing System for their structures. Houses built with the fibrous bricks cost less than others and yet were stronger and better insulated. The business grew and Bucky moved from place to place building new factories.

Anne, too, was busier than ever. With the death of her mother in 1923, she took on the care of the younger ones in her family. While the days were full with work, the nights were too long and empty for Bucky. When he was far from the Hewlett home and Anne, the depression over Alexandra's death would keep him awake. Often, he drank steadily all night long to blot out his pain and sorrow. With his incredible energy he could still go to work the next day. He worked twelve, fourteen hours a day and did a good job.

When Bucky had to supervise the building of a new factory in Illinois, he took an apartment in Chicago. His loneliness ended in 1926 when Anne, finally free from her family obligations, joined him. The apartment, located in one of the tall hotels on the shores of Lake Michigan, was a pretty and spacious one. From the windows Bucky could look down on the handsome yachts in the basin below.

Who would have dreamed that he would end up in Chicago, very near where Grandma Andrews lived as a girl? What would those head-shaking, disapproving uncles say if they could see him now? Even they would have to admit that the wild Fuller boy had come a long way. Only thirty-one years old, he headed a company with five factories. An inventor, he held two valuable patents: one for the system of framing the blocks, the other for the machinery that molded them. He had built over two hundred buildings already. (The University of Illinois used Fuller's blocks in the walls of one of its buildings.) He was meeting and dealing with important businessmen and powerful bankers. Only one faint worry nagged at him now. Mr. Hewlett had had financial problems. To get some needed cash, his father-in-law had sold his shares in the Stockade Building System to outsiders. But no one had interfered yet with Bucky's running of the business.

When Anne told him her good news, Bucky's spirits went sky-high. A new baby was due in August. Through the spring and summer of 1927, Bucky could feel the awful depression of the last five years begin to fade away. He worked harder than ever, ignored the stifling summer heat, and waited impatiently for August. The month had come almost to an end when, at last, on August 28, a small but perfect baby girl was born to the Fullers.

Walking into the Chicago Lying-In Hospital, Bucky was the happiest of men. That popular song, "Happy Days Are Here Again," might have been written just for him. As he looked down at Anne, a soaring joy and love filled his heart. Her long hair was loose on the pillow, framing her face and the brilliant smile on it. Anne proposed Allegra for the new baby's name.

Al-le-gra. It rolled musically from the lips. An Italian word, it means joyful, gay. In both sound and meaning, no better name could describe what the baby's coming meant to Bucky and Anne. Her birth seemed like a miracle, a second chance for happiness.

6   If Bucky was totally happy with his personal world, he was daily less satisfied with his business life. His aim was to build better housing for more people. Most of the world's people were still poorly housed. Even in America, only a small percentage of the *new* housing had indoor plumbing! Bucky did not care much whether the company profits increased rapidly. A new board of directors disagreed; these men wanted the company to earn more money faster than before and made business decisions accordingly. Despite these differences, Bucky was taken by surprise when the board of directors called him in. The single statement which they delivered struck him like a blow:

"Your services are no longer needed."

He was pushed out of the company. Fired. Most companies give either notice ahead of time or extra pay for firing without warning. Bucky got neither. Somehow, a stunned Bucky made his way home to the apartment and Anne. He should have known better than to ignore the businessman's love of money. What a fool he had been to follow his own ideas. Especially at this time when the new baby and Anne depended upon him.

As he finished telling Anne the news, he looked down at those clever hands with the long curving thumbs. It seemed as if everything he touched came to a bad end. The only words to describe himself were a "black, horrendous mess," he concluded bitterly. An unruffled Anne disagreed. Bucky's shoulders stayed hunched up in despair. How could he make her understand? There was more here than being fired. In the business world, he was discredited; no one would hire a man who neglected the goal of making money. Bucky had never been good at saving money, so they were penniless besides.

Sleepless nights followed restless days as he tried to sort out what to do next. His despair pushed him out of the apartment and into the streets of Chicago. He crossed boulevards packed with lines of honking cars, passed under the clattering, roaring elevated railways, and walked through leafy-green, bird-filled parks. Richard Buckminster Fuller saw and heard nothing.

He was haunted by the question: "Am I an utter failure?"

On one of those endless walks, he found himself on the shore of Lake Michigan at midnight. A cold wind blew. Looking into the black waters of the lake, he could see one solution. He could, very simply, jump in the lake, kill himself. If nothing else, that would give Anne and Allegra a chance to find someone better able to take care of them. His stern New England conscience told him that such a decision was, perhaps, a too-easy way out. What *are* the choices, Bucky asked himself. The only other choice was . . . to think. And Bucky began thinking harder than ever before in his life. Having lost his job, money, and reputation, what did he have left?

He said to himself, "I have *faith* . . . in the . . . wisdom which we may call 'God.' "

The questions flew into his mind and the answers came haltingly.

"Do I know best or does God know best whether I may be of any value to the integrity of the universe?"

"You don't know and no man knows. . . ." But, he concluded, "You do not have the *right* to eliminate yourself, you do not belong to you. You belong to the universe. . . . You and all men are here for the sake of other men."

Bucky straightened up and looked out into his universe. The shining stars looked like newly punched holes in the sky. In devoting the rest of his life to something greater than he was, he believed that his own life would straighten itself out.

Years later, in recalling that "pinch point of pain" and crisis in his life, Bucky wrote, "I did have many more types of experience than most . . . just by the good luck of being fired out of *this* and forced into *that* pattern. . . . So I had to do something about looking my experience over."

Trust Bucky Fuller to call being fired "good luck."

"And, if these experiences are put in order, they might be of use to others. . . . Whether I like it or not, I am the caretaker of a vital resource: me!"

He would try to convert all his experiences to the benefit of others.

In Bucky's planned research program, there was neither room nor time "to earn a living." He seemed to feel that the Lord would provide. Few men have been so fortunate in their marriages as Bucky Fuller. Anne accepted his stubborn faith and the changes in their life style with her usual serenity. They moved to a tiny, shabby apartment on Belmont Street in a neighborhood of poor people and run-down buildings. If Bucky gave her a dollar for food, then Anne made do with that single dollar. Some of their meals were slim ones, but there was always something on the table each day. Where did those little dribs and drabs of money come from? A relative died, leaving them a small amount of money; an old friend stopped by to repay a loan. Somehow, in one way or another, their needs were taken care of. The Lord or Providence did, indeed, provide.

Even more startling was the change in Bucky himself. Talkative, fun-loving, partying Bucky cut himself off from his friends and withdrew into almost total silence. It was not the silence of depression or despair but, rather, a planned part of his program. He had decided that "the way [he] had acquired bad rules and conflicting thoughts was through *words*." He had been too willing to believe what others asked him to believe. As he has put it, "I became very suspicious of words." Words are obviously tools, and he was enough of a mechanic to know that you can use tools in the wrong way.

Bucky changed not only his speaking habits but also his sleeping habits. He had noticed that when a dog gets tired it simply lies down and sleeps. The dog does not wait for a "bedtime" or night. Also, when it wakes, the dog springs into action with all energies available. Could it be that if a man lay down the minute that he was tired, he would need far less sleep? Bucky tried out his idea. Whenever he felt his concentration slipping, he would drop off for a half-hour nap. It worked. Out of each twenty-four hours, he slept only two or three hours altogether. So he had more than twenty hours each day to read, think, and put facts and experiences together.

For information, he turned to the public libraries of Chicago. Since he rarely had a dime in his pocket for bus fare, he walked to the nearest branches, and sometimes even farther to the main library. He studied an extraordinary variety of subjects and authors from the geographer Mackinder to the scientist Einstein. Strange as his actions seemed, he was following in the footsteps of other great thinkers. Thoreau, Descartes, Gandhi —each had retreated from the world to do his own thinking.

Meanwhile, friends and family once again shook their heads over Bucky's "irresponsible" behavior. For heaven's sake, what was Bucky *thinking about?* Anne, who made all his contacts with the outside world, explained his purpose and defended his actions fiercely. For man's sake, Bucky was thinking about the heavens, the whole of the universe, and man's place in it.

Centuries ago, a man named Thomas Malthus worked out the idea that the world's population was multiplying too fast. Malthus said (and used mathematics to prove it) that the food supply could not keep up with the increasing number of people. A natural conclusion to this was that only the strongest would survive. Many people accepted this picture of a "you-*or*-me" world; many governments operated on the belief that there wouldn't be enough to go around.

Against Malthus's ideas, Bucky weighed what he knew about the history of mankind and the basic patterns of Nature. Man was so perfectly designed to fit in this universe that Bucky refused to believe that Nature meant him to be a failure. He suspected that scientists had already developed the skills or know-how to meet all needs, present and future.

In wartime, people used every bit of knowledge they had of science, chemistry, and mathematics to win battles. They spent millions and billions of dollars developing new weapons, new transports, and new tools. Electric light bulbs and refrigerators

Portrait of Bucky, 1928, by Anne Fuller

first came into common use on battleships. Only afterward did
the rest of the world benefit from such advances.

What would happen if society applied the highest technology
directly to making man a success on earth? Was anyone working toward that goal? The mayor of a city plans around this
year's budget; the president of a company worries about next
spring's profits while the governor of a state campaigns for next

fall's election. Neither governments nor businesses care about such a far-off goal. But wasn't it nonsense to think that one man with no money and no credit could help bring about a world of "you-*and*-me" in which all human needs were met?

By asking himself such questions, Bucky was organizing his experiences and ideas. For months, he continued to exercise his own special method of "thinking." He devoted every waking moment to this effort. Even on the long walks pushing Allegra in her baby carriage through Lincoln Park, he carried on silent dialogues with himself. He did not then find all the answers, nor does he claim to have them all even today. But, as one admirer pointed out: "The genius of Richard Buckminster Fuller is that he knows exactly what questions to ask and in what order [to ask them]."

Answering the question of whether one man can be effective, Bucky drew on his experiences with boats and planes. A ship does not change course by its bow but by its rudder at the stern. The rudders have a little trim tab on the edge. By moving the trim tab in one direction, you can build a low pressure that pulls the whole around. There was no doubt in his mind. The individual can be a trim tab that turns the whole ship of state around with almost no effort at all.

Bucky Fuller was a practical man. In exploring what one person could do, he resolved never to spend any of his time trying to reform people. Rather than a reformer, he decided to be a "new former." He chose to work through the science of design on the problems of man's surroundings. Of all human needs, one of the greatest is shelter. Yet, he noted, it is among the last to receive scientific attention. The problems of shelter met all his requirements for action. He would be working on problems that no one else was working on and in a field that he knew well. By applying the latest scientific knowledge to house-building, he was sure that he could do more with less to everybody's benefit.

Bucky was not only thinking, he was also writing furiously. He wrote two thousand pages in that winter of 1927. The essay, *4D*, contained most of his basic ideas. Since he himself paid for the printing of two hundred copies, he cut down and crammed the work into less than fifty pages. Some readers found it "scholarly"; most found it cloudy and confusing. A man who invents his own words and gives new meanings to others was bound to be confusing. (He renamed architecture, calling it "environmental designing." "Livingry" is Bucky's single word to describe all the machines, tools, and things which keep people alive and well.)

Years ago, Bucky had invented a character called Spongee. According to Bucky, Spongee discovered America long before Columbus. In witty verse, Bucky had created a whole family for Spongee and drawn a fine, carefully detailed sketch of Spongee's ship. (The black-and-white sketch hangs today on a wall in the den of the Pierce home.) This private myth or joke, shared with his friend Linc Pierce, had been Bucky's "discovery of the past." In 1927, the essay, *4D*, and the plans which he drew were his first attempts to share with others his serious "discovery of the future." Many people dismissed his designs for the future as a joke and labeled Bucky a "charming nut." Forty-five years later, time proved Bucky's vision to be a true one.

What did his plans show that was so strange and different? Among other things, he designed lightweight buildings that could be "planted like trees."

For hundreds of years, men have built houses by piling up stones or bricks, one on top of another. Gravity pulling the top stones down holds them tightly together. Meanwhile, the bottom stone or brick must withstand the crushing weight of the ones above. The force pushing back is called compression. In walls built up that way, compression works vertically and tends to pull things apart. To carry loads in compression, men had to choose those building materials that would best resist crushing or being pulled apart.

Conventional houses with bricks piled up to support the roof and other parts are almost pure examples of compression-strength structures. Very few houses or structures ever used the

Above: a brick house shows compression strength; below: the Golden Gate Bridge in San Francisco is supported by a combination of compression and tension

tensile or pulled-taut strength of materials, a strength that exists along with compression strength. One exception to this is the tent or tepee, which depends for support on the tensile strength of its lightweight materials.

Suspension bridges like the Golden Gate Bridge are a partnership of these two kinds of strength. Towers carry the compressive load while the steel wire cables hung in tension support the roadway. (These cables demonstrate that tension works horizontally and can be made to hold things together.)

Bucky understood these principles of building and facts of engineering. He knew, too, that technology was constantly improving the tensile strength of materials. Even at that time, some metals and alloys had greater strength when used in tension than in compression. For his own house, he looked to the new aircraft industry where designers were using both kinds of strength to the greatest advantage. In their structures, the framework (in compression) was tied together by metal alloy cables (in tension). Thus, they created the strongest possible structures with the least possible weight. Like an airplane, the Fuller buildings were designed to have compression parts (a central mast) and tension parts (suspended walls and decks) separated out, re-

In Fuller's new design, single decks in the shape of hexagons (left) would be hung from a central mast (right)

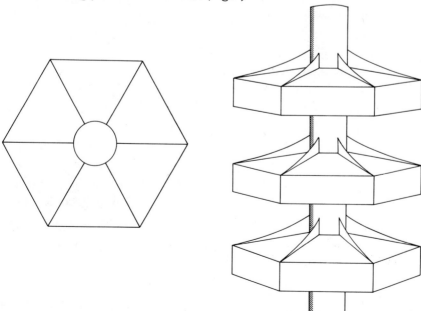

sulting in the same advantage. Another way to understand the idea behind Fuller's design is to picture a simple wire wheel of a bicycle turned over to rest on its hub rather than its rim. The hub then acts as a mast.

"Toward a New Architecture" read the caption over the newspaper sketch of a fantastic-looking structure. Readers of the accompanying article in the *Chicago Evening Post* learned that:

> These new homes are structured after the natural sys-
> tem of humans and trees with a central stem or back-
> bone from which all is independently hung. . . .

Drawings showed a ten-deck building that hung from a central, trunklike mast. The tower building, a blend of the American skyscraper and the oriental hexagonal pagoda, looked something like a six-sided tree. Since the floors and ceilings were supported by cables, the walls of the entire house could be transparent or opaque, giving it an airy, crystalline look. All the machinery to make the building work—plumbing, wiring for electricity, and generators—was already assembled (before construction) in the mast itself. The largest standard one-mast model included a swimming pool that ringed the building in the outer rim of one deck. Other decks contained a gymnasium, hospital, library; some were labeled "decks of necessity."

Buckminster Fuller wrote that article, which appeared on December 18, 1928, and gave the general public the imaginative results of his thinking. An exhibition of models and drawings by well-known European and American architects was to open in Chicago within the next month. Fuller, who had had no architectural training whatsoever, dared to suggest that *his* sketch might be "termed a *universal design.*"

Actually, he was offering more than a new-style apartment building or house; he was proposing a whole new industry. He had figured out that two billion new homes would be needed by the end of the century. Old methods of building could never keep up with the demands of an ever-increasing population. Instead of hammering together houses one-by-one on each site, Bucky suggested a revolutionary new way to build. All the parts of his apartment houses would be made in factories just as automobiles and airplanes were. He estimated that to develop this new industry and the factories would cost a billion dollars.

Fuller's sketch and notes compare his 4D tower house with a conventional six-room house

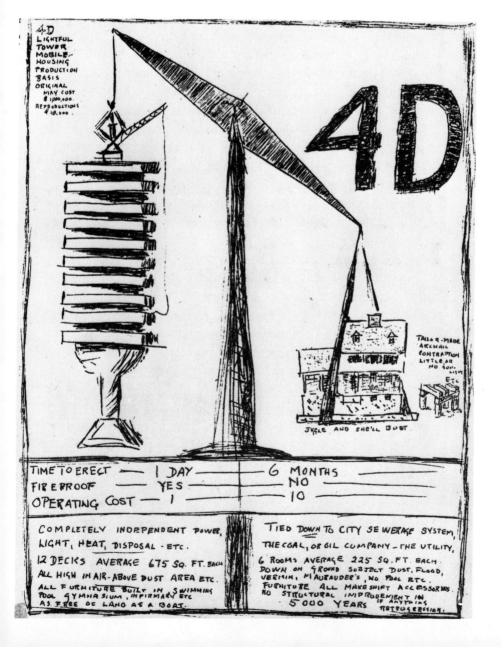

How to deliver these fully assembled buildings? It is not very practical to move thousands and thousands of house trailers through crowded city streets. Nor could such loads squeeze through narrow tunnels and under low bridges, It is practical, however, to carry them through the air, which is free and clear from obstacles. So he designed his towers to have minimum weight but maximum strength. He planned to make delivery by zeppelins, those huge cigar-shaped airships.

Approaching the building site, the dirigible or zeppelin would throw out an anchor to steady itself and drop a bomb to make a hole for the foundation. Then, "down comes the 4D tower house from the sky. Featherweight." After being lowered into the hole, the tower would be tied in with cables; concrete poured around the foundation would make it secure. "Off goes the zep to make a few more deliveries," Fuller wrote. His note underlined the speed with which a sky-scraping tower could be put up. Like the telephone company, this new service industry would "install" a building anywhere at a day's notice.

Besides "universal design," Bucky had still another conclusion and plan, his eye-opening idea of an "Air Ocean World Town Plan." Three quarters of the earth is water. Of the one quarter that is land, very little has been lived on by man. Fuller wrote, "Trees have roots, men have legs." As a creature designed to move, man should be able to shelter anywhere in the world.

Following this idea to its natural end, Bucky designed structures that did not need the mechanical services and support of a city. Each building was independent, capturing the wind for power, the sun for heat and light. No building had to be hooked up to sewer or electric power lines. Making delivery by air eliminated the need for roads or highways. With a streamlined plastic shield to surround and protect them from hostile weather and environment, these buildings could be planted anywhere from the Alaskan coast to the Sahara.

Man had been crowding into 5 percent of the dry spots on earth. If people could live anywhere on the globe, there might be space enough for that ever-increasing population.

Some people took Fuller's ideas seriously. With their financial help, Bucky formed the 4D Company to continue his work. He rented a post office box, prepared patent applications, and found students to help him build models. For her part, Anne took care of the daily chores of living. Carrying in the groceries, taking out the garbage, she often had the help of a neighbor. When Anne spied a gun under the man's jacket, she made no comment. Neighbors on Belmont Street did not ask one another questions. He might be a gangster working for a Chicago mob, but he was polite and helpful to her. She was more concerned with keeping Allegra from harm and danger spots like the hot stove and the elevator shaft. Rather than say "no, no" every minute of the day, Anne found clever ways to draw Allegra's attention elsewhere. Bucky admired Anne's way of encouraging Allegra to develop freely with safety. He was less admiring of the time Anne had to spend cleaning up the day's dirt and trash.

When he scaled down the ten-deck building to a design for a one-family house, he offered solutions to these problems of daily safety and constant cleaning. The one-family house, too, was hung by tension cables from a central mast. To an amazing degree, his "scientific dwelling machine" harnessed the natural energies of the sun and wind. Lenses in the mast collected and used the light and heat of the sun, while a central pipe carried rain water through the mast. Up top, a windmill caught breezes to operate the power generator. Air coming in through vents in the central mast was cleaned, cooled or heated, and then circulated through the house. Air-conditioned, dustless, sound-proof—this machine for living almost took care of itself.

Working as a comprehensive designer, Bucky asked himself questions that never occurred to the architects of his day. A typical question was: What do people use water for? He knew that each American was then using two hundred gallons per day. Only one gallon a day was used for eating and drinking. The other one hundred and ninety-nine gallons were spent "to dunk themselves, and gadgets, and to act as a . . . system for carrying specks of dirt to the sea." All of this led him to the

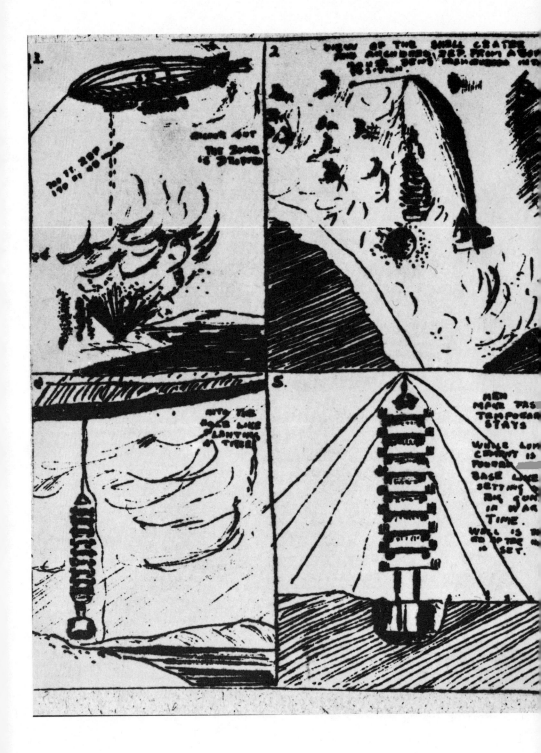

*Fuller's drawings show
a zeppelin delivery of
a 4D tower house*

next question: "Are there not superior ways to effect many of the end purposes involving no water at all? . . ." And the next: "Where water is found to be essential can it not be separated out? . . ."

His inventive conclusion was that a person using his "fog gun" could shower in just *one quart* of water. And that quart of water would be collected, filtered, sterilized, and used again.

In the 4D House, machines did all the work automatically. His dishwasher not only cleaned and dried the dishes but also put them away in the cupboards. All the closets had shelves that revolved mechanically. A central vacuum system and compressed air would do whatever cleaning needed to be done. Freed from the drudgery of daily chores, people could educate themselves in the go-ahead-with-life room. A kind of library, that room would hold maps, globes, revolving bookshelves, and a radio-television receiver (something not yet developed).

Many of the machines and materials designed into his house had not yet been invented. But they were not wild science fiction drawn just from his imagination. He based them on his experiences and research, experimental models, and known scientific ideas. He was convinced, for example, that light energy could be converted into electrical energy. Perhaps, by interrupting a light beam with a wave of the hand, doors and windows could be opened automatically. In 1927, Bucky had written to his brother Wolcott, an engineer with General Electric, and asked if anyone was working out this idea.

In answer, Wolcott wrote: "Bucky, I love you dearly. But can't you make it easier for your relatives and friends by not including your preposterous ideas?"

A telegram came for Bucky just one year later. The telegram was from Wolcott and said:

YOU CAN OPEN YOUR DOOR BY WAVING YOUR HAND AFTER ALL STOP WE HAVE DEVELOPED PHOTOELECTRIC CELL AND RELAY STOP SEVENTY-TWO DOLLARS FOR THE SET STOP.

Today many supermarkets, banks, and businesses use electrically opened doors.

Bucky met the same reaction when he talked with the engineers about the aluminum he needed for his central mast. The mast had to be lightweight but strong. In 1928, aluminum

Model of a ten-deck 4D house surrounded by a plastic shield

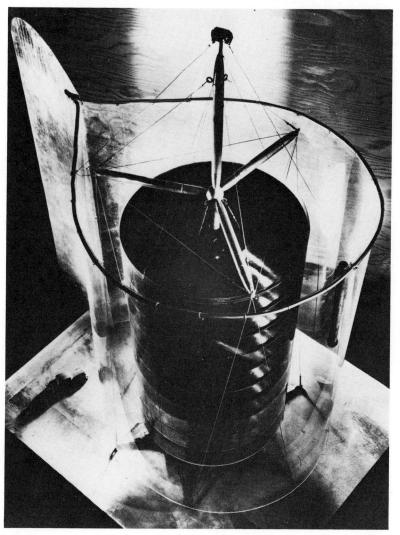

was used only for things like pots, ashtrays, and cheap trinkets. An engineer's irritated reply was, "We have two kinds of aluminum: soft and softer. Which kind do you want?" Only an idiot would talk then about using aluminum for buildings. But five years later the heat-treated alloys of aluminum that Bucky was looking for became widely available.

Bucky Fuller was neither surprised nor dismayed by such reactions from the people he approached. By deliberate choice, he was working roughly fifty years ahead of his time. He had measured the gaps between when an invention or discovery was made and when it got put to use as a practical tool. In radio, it took two years; in the airplane industry, five years. For the housing industry to put either new methods or machines into use would take at least forty-five years.

In 1972, a conversation with a business leader proved Bucky's timetable right.

The community leader said, "We've got a new industry coming to East St. Louis. I suppose you've heard about it. . . ."

"What is it?"

"Mass production of bathrooms."

Was there the ghost of a smile on Fuller's face? He answered, "They are right on time. I designed the first one forty-five years ago."

7 Meanwhile, in April 1928 Bucky completed his designs and applied for patents to protect his ideas. Besides publishing the book *4D*, he built a three-foot model of his "scientific dwelling machine." Thanks to the newspaper articles and the exhibit, people were beginning to talk about R. Buckminster Fuller.

Now at last Bucky was ready to start talking. A short, chunky figure carrying his model in a bulky suitcase, he went eagerly anywhere and everywhere that he was invited. Would Mr. Fuller show his model at the Chicago Home Owners' Exhibition? Gladly. Appearances there marked the beginning of his lifelong series of lectures. Some say that to make up for his long silence, Bucky Fuller hasn't stopped talking since. He has been clocked at speaking seven thousand words an hour and has been known to lecture for six hours at a time.

The 4D House—in fact all of Fuller's designs in that period of time—came to be known as "Dymaxion" designs. Oddly enough, that trademark was invented by someone else. When the Marshall Field department store in Chicago set up a display of modern furniture, a store official remembered Fuller's "house of the future." What better way to draw attention to their modern furniture and to make it look less startling than to show Fuller's model alongside?

The advertising man who came to discuss the display with Bucky shook his head over the name "4D House." It could mean anything from a failing grade in school to a room number in a hotel. Bucky was reluctant to give up the name "4D"; he had chosen it to represent the fourth dimension. But he could see the advertising man's point. To catch people's attention, a more dramatic name was needed. While Bucky explained his designs and the ideas behind them, the advertising man listened and made notes. From these notes, he took certain words that kept appearing over and over. Then, using syllables from those words, he created a series of synthetic words. Together, the two men went over the list discarding, recombining, and agreeing finally on one word as the most attractive. The winner,

"Dy-max-i-on," was a combination from the words: "dynamic," "maximum," and "ion." Since the trademark was registered in Fuller's name, the right to use that word belongs to him alone. Today in people's minds everywhere, the names R. Buckminster Fuller and Dymaxion are linked together like salt and pepper. They cannot think of one without the other.

Despite Fuller's lack of training as an architect, a few young architects were willing to listen to him. One of these young men had a car. In June of 1929, Bucky and this friend drove down to St. Louis. The American Institute of Architects was holding its convention there. His friend managed to set up the house model on the convention floor. In keeping with his principles of helping humanity, Bucky had planned to make a gift of his patent rights to the Institute. Most of the delegates walked away from his exhibit and some denounced him with an angry storm of words. The Board of the Institute of Architects not only rejected his generous offer but also voted to put itself "on record as . . . opposed to any peas-in-a-pod designs."

No one objects to mass-produced books or mass-produced cars. Why did these architects reject even the idea of mass-produced houses? Did they think perhaps that people living in identical houses would be forced to live identical lives? Many people in a city have identical pianos, but they do not all play the same piece of music at the same time on their pianos.

In those supposedly different-looking or "individual" houses that architects designed, people were in fact all tied to doing the same housekeeping jobs over and over. In Bucky's Dymaxion House, the house and its machines did those jobs. People freed from silly daily chores would have the time and the choice of what to do.

Perhaps the architects saw the Dymaxion House as a threat to their earnings. The most basic 4D design would provide more conveniences and luxuries at less cost than any architect-designed house. In any case, the final victory was Bucky's, for in 1970 this same Institute awarded its highest prize, a gold medal, to that nonarchitect, R. Buckminster Fuller.

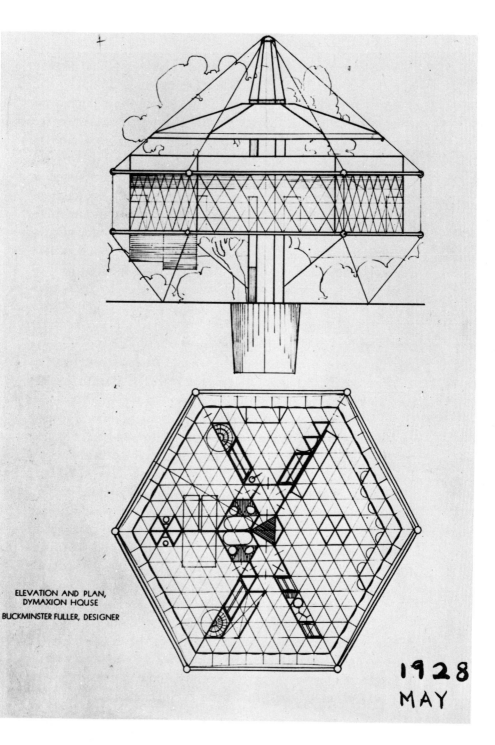

ELEVATION AND PLAN,
DYMAXION HOUSE
BUCKMINSTER FULLER, DESIGNER

1928
MAY

While the award recognized his contributions, the housing industry has yet to accept his scientific approach. As Bucky had observed in 1927, society accepts new ideas and uses the highest technology only for military or defense purposes. When the United States engaged in a race against the Soviet Union to land men on the moon, the people in charge of the project followed Bucky's footsteps. The spaceship architects aimed at lightness rather than heaviness and worked with the laws of nature. Instead of starting with existing materials, they first designed the spaceship and *then* hunted for and developed new materials to carry out the design. Self-contained, making its own heat and light, pumping its own water and disposing of its own waste, the spaceship is a scientifically planned shelter that takes care of every physical need of a human. Perhaps another forty years will see Bucky's vision of the scientifically planned shelter come true for men on earth as well as on the moon.

In July of 1929, an article in the *Chicago Evening Post* summed up the results of Bucky's effort. The director of the Academy of Fine Arts wrote, "Chicago has in the mass disregarded that very latest development, the house hung from a central mast . . . a design which upsets all our ideas of period styles in design." He predicted, however, that the world would hear more of that model.

Two years of hard thinking, writing, and explaining had left Bucky more than ready for a vacation. So the Fullers joined the other members of the family on Bear Island for the summer. Nothing on the island had changed from his boyhood days; only the trees had grown taller. Bucky took great satisfaction in the unchanging way of life on the island and welcomed the hard work that went with it. On the beach little Allegra played with a crowd of cousins, while on the boats Roger Hewlett, Anne's brother, lent a hand with scrubbing down the decks. From the plunges into the cold bay waters to the wind whistling down the fireplace chimney at night, Bucky enjoyed every minute of each day. Once again, Bear Island gave Bucky the chance to use his body and mind to the fullest and he found himself refreshed and renewed. At the end of the summer he, Anne, and a toddling, talkative Allegra moved to New York. With his wife and daughter settled out on Long Island, Fuller tackled New York City. Surely in New York he could find a marketplace for his ideas.

Few people caught the hints or saw the clues pointing to the disaster that was coming in the fall of 1929. For the last part of the twenties, people from all walks of life had turned to the stock market as a way of getting rich quickly. Using savings and borrowing money, they bought stocks or shares in companies at low prices, waited briefly for the price to rise, sold at a profit, and then bought still more stocks. The center for this trading and buying was on Wall Street in New York City.

In October of that year, the "Great Crash" occurred. Banks, companies, and people had lost confidence in the value of the stocks that they were buying and selling. Everyone tried to sell at once. Prices went down and still nobody would buy; the shares of stock became worthless pieces of paper. Banks called in their loans and people could not repay. In the panic that followed, the whole system of business and industry broke down. Factories closed; banks shut their doors; people lost their savings and jobs. America was in a great business depression.

Bucky, Allegra and Anne in Lincoln Park, Chicago, 1928, when Allegra was learning to walk

Recalling those Depression days after the Crash, Bucky says, "Those were the days when hordes [of people] slept on the floors of subway stations. Some restaurants were down to one-cent meals. You could buy a suit of clothing for a dollar. Even then, nobody could sell anything; nobody had any money [to buy with]."

Like many others in those extraordinary times, Bucky Fuller had no regular business and no regular income. For himself, he needed very little money. The little that he earned from lecturing and showing his Dymaxion House model went to support Anne and Allegra. He lived a wandering, gypsylike life and, oddly enough, the place where he spent much of his time was at a gypsy's restaurant, Romany Marie's in that part of New York City known as Greenwich Village.

At Romany Marie's, thinkers, artists, and authors all came together to talk. When Romany Marie had to move her restaurant, she asked Bucky to decorate the new place on Minetta Lane. Not surprisingly, Bucky created an imaginative modern design with huge aluminum cones throwing a bright indirect light. Bucky not only planned the decoration, he also made every bit of the new furniture with his own hands.

Romany Marie could not afford to pay Bucky in cash. Instead she promised, "I'll give you a meal every day." On the stove she kept a big soup pot cooking all the time. Adding vegetables, little pieces of meat from time to time, a little more water made the taste-base well seasoned, thick, and delicious.

Bucky still remembers those meals: "The soup and black bread were wonderful and you finished with a stewed-fruit compote and Turkish coffee."

Who could ask for anything more? But Bucky did not want to take advantage of Marie's offer. With typical independence and stubbornness, he tried to eat there only every other day. Often he would stay all evening long with only a cup of coffee. As a "table sitter" in Romany Marie's, Bucky drew in customers who came just to hear him talk. Then, as now, it did not matter to Bucky whether there was a crowd or only one person listening to him. He talked just as intently for any size audience.

"It was there," Bucky points out, "that I learned to think out loud in public." He adds that this "thinking-out-loud" produces sudden and unexpected truths. Perhaps this explains why so many people come in such numbers and stay so many hours at his lectures today.

He walked everywhere, from Greenwich Village over the Brooklyn Bridge and back to uptown Manhattan, delivering lectures to any and all who would listen. The world was both hearing about and seeing more of his Dymaxion House, just as had been predicted.

In those moneyless times, he landed one steady job that lasted for six months. The president of the American Radiator and Standard Sanitary Company liked Fuller's ideas enough to test them for practicality. He gave Bucky money and staff to turn out a real working model of the bathroom designed for the Dymaxion House. Bucky produced a one-piece bathroom that could be made in a factory and hooked up in a house just like a stove or refrigerator. Although the model was a success, the company never manufactured it.

In Fuller's own words: "The manufacturer was convinced that the plumbers' union would refuse to install the bathroom." By his own calculations, it would take another forty years before the building industry would be willing to accept such a revolutionary idea. The experiment remained just that, and Bucky's temporary job came to an end.

Neither the loss of his job nor lack of money bothered Bucky. As far as he is concerned, real wealth is not money or the gold buried under Fort Knox. Real wealth is energy which never leaves the Universe and knowledge which can only increase always. And he was happily busy increasing his own and the world's knowledge.

In the spring of 1930, Bucky and his sculptor friend Isamu Noguchi loaded a station wagon for a trip to Chicago. Noguchi

Above: Fuller with a model of the Dymaxion House. At right, top: the kitchen of a Dymaxion house that was built later (1941); bottom: a Dymaxion bathroom, shown with the top half removed (1938)

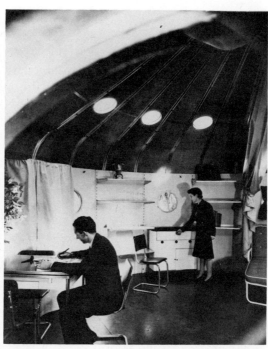

had been invited to show eighteen pieces of sculpture at the Arts Club, while Bucky planned to exhibit his Dymaxion House at the annual show of the Architectural League. Stuffed as it was with bronze heads and a "hanging house," the station wagon presented a strange sight for other drivers on the road.

Although the weekend was cool and rainy, the reception of their work was warm and enthusiastic. Describing Noguchi's exhibit of bronze heads, one reporter called it a "knock-out show." And the architecture writer for the *Chicago Evening Post* called Fuller's house a "very beautiful thing." That reporter commented on the safety as well as the beauty of the house:

> If little Willie falls out of bed for instance, he won't hurt himself, because the floor will be pneumatic [air-filled like a balloon] and he'll bounce.

She added the hope that there would be a life-sized Dymaxion House at the Chicago World's Fair in 1933.

The architecture committee had, indeed, approached Bucky with the idea of featuring his house at the Fair. Fuller agreed on the condition that the display would not be just another larger size model or "mock-up." Rather, he wanted to develop a true "prototype" (the first working house), fully engineered and ready to roll off the assembly line.

"How much will it cost?" the World's Fair committee asked.

"I will have to recheck my figures and let you know," Bucky replied.

A prototype—the first of its kind—is always fantastically expensive. The high cost of making the first one includes the high cost of learning how to do it. To manufacture a prototype, machinery for making it has to be developed as well. When ball-point pens were first made in quantity thirty years ago, they sold for thirty dollars each. Now they are so cheap to make that they are given away free to advertise businesses or candidates.

Fuller worked out his costs the way the automobile industry did—by what it cost per pound. If his house could be mass-produced, the price would be twenty-five cents a pound or at a total cost to the customer of fifteen hundred dollars. (Fords and Chevrolets at that time sold for twenty-two cents a pound.) For a house like Fuller's, fully equipped, this was a sensationally cheap price. Since he had made his first estimates, new discoveries and materials had been developed. So his new figures would be considerably less than his original billion-dollar figure.

Meeting again with the promoters, Bucky told them, "The basic cost today is a hundred million dollars."

One of his friends has said that Bucky could "persuade a silkworm that nylon is better," but in this case his persuasive powers failed. To these men, who wanted simply an exhibit for the Fair, Fuller's figures were a jolt. They did not understand that Bucky Fuller was offering them a whole new industry. Bucky's idea was so sane as to seem insane to most. Certainly the World's Fair people thought they were dealing with a lunatic, and they promptly abandoned the idea of a Dymaxion House.

Bucky wasted no time in regrets. What was done was done. He concentrated now on getting people to think about the merging of science and architecture. Some young architects were listening to him, but he needed to reach a wider audience. Cashing in his insurance policies in 1930, he scraped together enough money to buy a magazine which he renamed *Shelter*.

Bucky's approach to the business part of publishing was startling, to say the least. He canceled all the contracts for paid advertising. In fact, he refused to print any ads at all. Since magazines make their money from the advertisements that appear in them, Bucky and *Shelter* were clearly headed for disaster.

But Bucky Fuller was very clear in his own mind about what he was doing and why. Advertising contracts require the publisher to bring out regular issues on regular dates. This means meeting deadlines. Bucky felt that "thinking" has its own timing and cannot be hurried to meet editorial deadlines. He notified all subscribers that they would receive issues when he felt deeply in need of saying something. Then he told them that for the luxury of saying *what* he thought needed to be said *when* he needed to say it, they could pay him two dollars a copy! (The most expensive magazine at that time charged one dollar a copy.)

People argued about *Shelter*, criticized its editor and his ideas, but they also bought it. Within months, the number of subscribers had multiplied incredibly. Even the well-established *Architectural Forum* could not boast of having more subscribers than *Shelter* did.

In *Shelter*, Bucky provided a place for creative architects, like Frank Lloyd Wright, to air their ideas. Bucky himself wrote, not just about shapes and kinds of shelter, but about the whole environment. His first "chapter" dealt with ecology, a word and subject that few people had heard or understood in the 1930's. Even today, when we accept the importance of ecology in our lives, Bucky's points startle the listener into new thinking.

"Earth is a tiny planet where energy is supposed to be stored and saved," says Bucky. He points out that pollution is really a *resource that is out of place* and argues that the resource of pollution should be "harvested." All the sulfur dioxide escaping from smokestacks equals the amount of sulfur being mined from the ground. Why not "mine" the smokestacks to reclaim the sulfur? In *Shelter*, pictures of smokestacks belching black clouds into the sky underlined his points.

Meanwhile, the country continued to suffer from the Great Depression. The stale, defeated air of the Depression clung to every business effort and every government proposal to create more jobs and money. But the brisk November winds of 1932 blew a new hope of change around the country. Franklin Delano Roosevelt, elected to the presidency of the United States, pledged himself to a "new deal" for the American people. The new President reminded all that the only thing they had to fear was fear itself.

To everyone's astonishment, just at this point, Bucky abruptly chose to shut down his magazine. "But why?" asked some people. Why close down just when the magazine was on its way to becoming a success? (What they really meant was why stop when *Shelter* was about to make money and a profit?) There should have been no surprise. Buckminster Fuller was the man who had chosen to ignore the need to earn a living in 1927; he was no different in 1932. Bucky's concern was for ideas, useful ones. With the election of F.D.R., he felt confident that the new government would concern itself with the needs of homes, new industry, and jobs for people. If so, it was time for him to push off in a new direction.

And the last issue of *Shelter* in November of 1932 showed the new direction that he wanted to explore. In that issue, readers saw the detailed drawings for a new kind of transport, an eye-catching transport with the streamlined shape of a raindrop.

8 In World War I, the winged flying machine had been transformed from an entertaining new toy to a serious weapon of war. Some naval officers, like Bucky's commanding officer, were early supporters of airplanes. Lt. Commander Patrick Bellinger, one of the Navy's first pilots, had traveled to Europe in 1914 to study the superior French and Italian planes.

Talking with Bellinger in 1917, the ever-curious Bucky had discussed the future uses and kinds of planes that would be developed in the years ahead. Clearly, the ships of the air would be navigating over the high seas just as the surface ships had. Which would be speedier and more stable, seaplanes or land planes? Or would there be some new kind of plane as yet undreamed of? The two men explored possibilities in long talks. Both the talks and the germ of an idea stayed in Bucky's mind for ten years.

Even as he sketched his Dymaxion House in 1927, Bucky Fuller asked himself more questions. If his Dymaxion House was to be planted anywhere in the world, on mountain tops or in deserts, how would people reach the house or leave it? Any vehicle a family used had to be independent of roads, rail lines, or runways. It should be able to taxi on both land and water. Again, Bucky looked to Nature for the principle which he would use.

Like a soaring sea gull, a moving airplane has the ability to create a low pressure area above its wings. This low-pressure area has the effect of a partial vacuum which must always be filled. As a result, the plane or gull gets "sucked skywards" or, in other words, gets a "lift." This same lift is what keeps gliders up in the air. But the duck has too small a wing to create enough of this kind of lift to support its weight. To rise up, the duck uses a kind of jet principle. Each thrust of its wings pushes out a powerful air jet between the wing and the body. Beating its wings furiously, the duck vaults skyward and forward on its own jet stream.

When he published the *4D* essay in 1928, Bucky included a sketch of his new transport idea. Later, for Allegra's benefit,

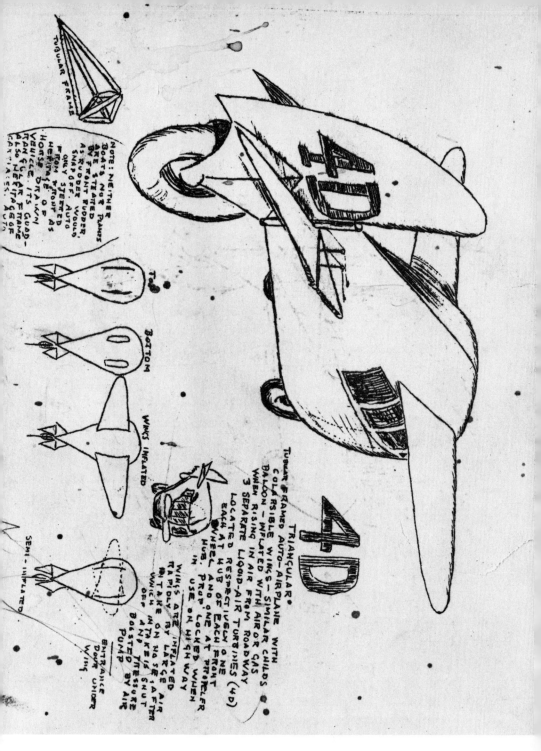

Fuller's sketches and notes on his zoomobile, or 4D transport, in 1927

he explained his invention as a "zoomobile." In Fuller's zoo-mobile, the power to lift and move the transport came from twin combustion plants, consisting of gas turbines, jets, and rocket thrusts. The zoomobile had all the freedom of a wild duck. An auto-airplane, it had collapsible wings which would inflate like a balloon as the vehicle rose into the air. It could take off from an airport, fly over fields and towns, and slip down again into the mainstream of highway traffic.

As with the house, the technology to make the transport possible did not yet exist. There were no metals or alloys of metals strong enough for his engines. The liquid fuel he proposed using created such intense heat that the engines would melt. And Bucky certainly did not have enough money then to carry out experiments or build a prototype.

Bucky knew that in time new metal alloys would be developed and could more or less predict the schedule. He knew, too, that the problems of maneuvering in the air would be solved more easily than other problems. Actually, the greatest unknowns and difficulties lay in the use of his wingless fish on the ground.

Having pinpointed the key problem, he bombarded it with questions: How would it taxi? . . . What would the winds do? . . . On icy fields would it . . . ?

Sketching steadily, Bucky created a design for the transport in its ground or car stage. Finally, he was ready to have the world look at it.

Travelers and tourists, businessmen, housewives, lawyers flowed in great streams in and out of New York's Grand Central train station. The crowds swelled even more in December. If they looked up over their heads, they could see the glorious murals of the heavens painted by Monroe Hewlett, Bucky's father-in-law. If they stopped scurrying and looked around, they could see Buckminster Fuller's work, too, for the Engineer's Bookshop had sponsored a display.

Christmas shoppers might be too busy to look, but in January at the National Automobile Show everyone's attention focused on the new cars and trucks displayed temptingly throughout the four floors of the Grand Central Palace. Brilliantly illuminated, the shining cars revolved slowly on turntables while pretty girls stood at the side explaining the new features. Newspapers reported on what drew the largest crowds: a bouncing, single cylinder 1902 Cadillac, and the "one car sprung as a surprise . . . designed along radical aerodynamic lines." With his models displayed in a featured booth at the show, Bucky Fuller needed nothing else to draw the crowds' attention.

Milling around, the crowds chattered excitedly:

"Is that what we're coming to?"

"Yes, so they say. . . ."

"It's gorgeous!"

"It doesn't seem like a car at all, does it?"

"We've come a long way, brother."

Shortly after, one of Bucky's friends and supporters offered him some money to test his Dymaxion ideas. Bucky accepted cautiously. He insisted on one condition: that he should be totally free to use the money in any way that he chose.

"If I want to use all of it to buy ice cream cones, that will be that, and there will be no questions asked," he said.

So it happened that Bucky Fuller in the midst of the Depression found himself holding several thousand dollars in cash.

For once, Bucky Fuller could pick and choose. What he chose to do was build a 4D transport to test its capabilities on the ground. Bucky began to line up the resources that he needed: a factory site, workers, tools. In Bridgeport, Connecticut, he found an ideal location. The old Locomobile Company had gone out of business, leaving an empty building for rent at a small sum. He found there also many skilled mechanics and craftsmen who had been left unemployed. A thousand or more men applied for the twenty-eight jobs that Bucky offered. In hiring, Bucky considered both a man's skill and his needs. Fuller picked those who needed work the most, those who had wives and children to feed. More than one of these men burst into tears of relief when hired.

To make the plaster models, he had called on his sculptor

friend Isamu Noguchi. Bucky then persuaded W. Starling Burgess (that fellow Milton Academy alumnus who had lectured there years ago) to become his chief engineer. Burgess brought with him the special experience of pioneer work with both boats and planes. He had invented the Delta-winged plane and designed the big yachts which won the America's Cup races.

In return for Burgess's help, Bucky promised to work with him on the building of a new kind of sloop. This project was added to the work of building the second transport: Both projects shared the same building space, workers, and the attention of the two men. According to Bucky, he worked on the stern, while Burgess took care of the bow. (Up at Bear Island, Bucky's sister Rosy was involved with the building of a new boat at the same time. Perhaps it was an example of the loving bond between these two. Perhaps it was ESP. Whatever it was, each, unknown to the other, chose the name *Little Dipper*.)

W. Starling Burgess at work on the 4D transport

Burgess and Fuller with the first Dymaxion car, July 12, 1933

On March 4, 1933, President Roosevelt took both his oath of office and action to restore confidence in the business and government of America. That same week, Bucky Fuller began the production of his 4D transport. Although he and Burgess might disagree on some engineering solution or design, they did share a certain point of view: "Never turn out a prototype that just works and proves a point. It must be magnificently executed . . . that is a pioneer's responsibility to society."

Italian machine-tool men, Polish sheet-metal experts, Scandinavian craftsmen—each worked with fine care to produce a perfectly finished piece. When the first working transport rolled out of the factory doors on July 12, 1933, excitement and pride soared even higher. Bucky Fuller was thirty-eight years old that day. Surely the sight of that gleaming aluminum, bullet-shaped object was the best birthday present Bucky had ever had!

Looking something like a submarine which has come up from the sea and something like a dirigible which has come down from the air, his creation resembled nothing ever seen on a road before. In his transport, the driver sat right up against the front of the car. There was no long hood to block his view. Aircraft-glass (shatterproof) windows wrapped around the front to give the driver the widest possible view of the road. Sticking up through the roof, the rear-view periscopes gave him an equally good view behind.

The low-bellied wingless fish rode on just three wheels, two in the front and one in the rear. Like the rudder on a ship, the single rear wheel did the steering. The two front wheels provided traction and braking, an important new safety feature. Fuller demonstrated to reporters with a toy baby carriage. With rear wheels locked, the baby carriage sliding along the floor skidded badly. When the front wheels were locked, the skidding was eliminated. "She was the most stable car in history," says Fuller.

The running gear was enclosed in the streamlined belly of the fuselage. This allowed all the interior space of the car to be used for the roomy comfort of the passengers. (The useful space inside was double that of the average car, and his second model could carry eleven people.)

So many new ideas went into that transport: front-wheel drive, air conditioning, recessed headlights, a rear engine.

The public had its chance to see how some of these new ideas worked, or in fact whether they worked at all. Nine days later, three thousand people packed the test track of the old Loco-mobile Company. Important people—a brigadier general, a major general from the Army Air Corps, the motor vehicle commissioner of Connecticut—came for the unveiling and test run.

Would the transport be able to reach the high speed which the designer predicted? Had the center of gravity been lowered enough? Would the car tip over at high speeds? Moments before the test run began were filled with anxious unspoken questions.

Bucky Fuller, as always, looked confident. The Dymaxion darted out onto the track. As smoothly as any airplane in the air, she sailed along on the ground at a speed of seventy miles an hour. Actually, the Dymaxion could easily do 120 miles an hour. Bucky, worried about the crowds hedged along the track, did not want to run her at top speed that day.

How could the Dymaxion travel so fast? To reach that speed an ordinary 1933 sedan would need an engine of over three hundred horsepower. Yet the Dymaxion did it with a regular Ford V-8 engine rated at ninety horsepower. The secret lay in the design.

Until the Dymaxion appeared, the shape of most cars was similar to the outline of a horse and closed wagon, with the motor taking the place of the horse. The old horse-drawn wagons moved so slowly that the problem of "air resistance" did not exist. Automobiles, however, move faster and come up against this problem in trying to speed through the air. Just as a person uses more energy to walk into a strong wind, a car's power gets used up trying to push through the air. Millions of invisible air particles rub against everything that moves through them. This rubbing is called friction and friction is a force that slows down moving objects.

At high speeds, almost 80 percent of an engine's power goes into fighting friction or "air resistance." Only 20 percent is left to provide speed. Most designers at that time tried to increase a car's speed simply by piling more and more power into the engine.

Bucky Fuller does not believe in conquering one force by using another force. He prefers to yield, coax, and adapt Nature's forces to go in the directions he prefers. By streamlining the Dymaxion's shape to resemble the fish which moves so easily through water, he reduced friction and increased the car's speed.

Everywhere the Dymaxion went, it created a sensation. Before Bucky's mother died in 1934, she had the pleasure of hear-

The shape of a standard 1932 automobile resembles the outline of a horse and closed wagon

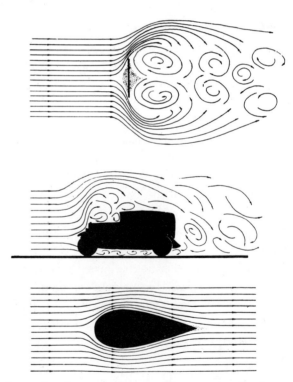

Fuller's sketches show the flow of air around a conventional car and around a streamlined form

ing the world praise her son's "genius." Engineers applauded his design and technology; reporters wrote admiringly of the smooth, floating ride and comfort.

Bucky could not resist the temptation of showing off the Dymaxion's advantages and specialties. One day he drove down Fifth Avenue with ten magazine editors as passengers. In those days, New York had traffic policemen rather than traffic lights on the corners of main streets. A puzzled policeman whistled the Dymaxion to a stop, asking what the heck this thing was. A mischievous Bucky not only explained the principles of the transport, but also gave him a quick demonstration of its ability to make tight turns. While he was talking, he rotated the car completely around the astonished policeman. Every policeman along Fifth Avenue stopped him to ask for a similar demonstration. That day it took over an hour for the Dymaxion to travel one mile! Traveling between New York and Washington, D.C., Bucky was stopped fifty-two times. Using different excuses, state and city policemen kept arresting him so they could haul the car into the station for a good look.

"She was able to behave in very spectacular ways," Fuller recalls with a smile.

The Dymaxion demonstrated its "ways" at the 1933 Chicago World's Fair. In the Wings of Century parade, every form of American transportation, from cowboys on horseback to puffing steam engines, passed in review. Last in the parade, a Dymaxion model would zoom across at forty-five miles an hour. When the car braked suddenly and spun around, the crowd in the stands would stand up with a gasp of horror. Each and every audience was convinced that the car would roll over on itself. Each and every time, the Dymaxion made the "impossible" turn, pivoting smartly around to the relieved cheers of the audience.

In every test, the car proved its superior design. The average car then needed twenty and a half feet of space in order to park. Even though the Dymaxion was four feet longer than average, it used only twenty feet to park. Instead of backing into a parking space, the car pointed its nose into the curb and the tail then whipped in sideways. This stunning beauty had another practical advantage: she got forty miles to a gallon of gas.

Why aren't there Dymaxions everywhere on the road today?

The spectacular car suffered a spectacular piece of bad luck. In 1933, the first Dymaxion model was in an accident just outside the Chicago World's Fair. The driver died and the passengers suffered serious injuries. When reporters arrived at the scene, they saw only the blood and wreckage of the Dymaxion and its passengers. The result was screaming headlines: "Freak Car Crashes" or "Dymaxion Car Kills Driver." Every article gave the impression that the car had some fatal fault; no article mentioned another car.

Disturbed, Bucky immediately flew to Chicago. A thorough examination of the Dymaxion showed nothing the matter with the car, either in the design or the construction.

When a hearing was held thirty days later to investigate the accident, the injured passengers had recovered enough to testify. Another car owned by a minor politician had tried to race the Dymaxion and rammed into it. Because of this politician's power and influence, the other car had been removed immediately. Although the truth came out at the hearing, the damage had been done by those first screaming headlines. The truth—an irresponsible driver crashing into another car—was too ordinary a happening to be considered "headline news." If any newspapers printed this evidence, the articles were too small and buried for anyone to notice.

An English company that had been interested in the Dymaxion backed away from putting any money into it.

With his strong sense of responsibility, Bucky felt obliged to remove the blame mistakenly attached to the Dymaxion. He plowed every bit of money from his mother's estate into building two more models to prove the car's complete reliability. Each model showed still more improvements in design. But it was not enough. Not even the pictures of Eleanor Roosevelt and Amelia Earhart riding in the Dymaxion could offset the bad publicity.

Dymaxion Car No. 3, completed in 1934

American car manufacturers had additional reasons for ignoring the Dymaxion. That year, Chrysler introduced its Air Flow model, supposedly a streamlined design. Next to Bucky's model, the Air Flow looked like a bad joke. With millions of dollars tied up in the new model, Chrysler took steps to avoid looking foolish. The company pressed officials of the Auto Show to exclude Bucky from his reserved space in the show. Bucky never backed away from a challenge of any kind. Driving his Dymaxion around the block, he parked it at the curb directly in front of the Grand Central Palace. There, it attracted more crowds and attention than anything inside the building.

Meeting with Fuller, Walter Chrysler, president of the company, admitted that Bucky had "designed the car that ought to be built."

But its revolutionary design would require the automobile industry to scrap almost every tool and die it had. Millions of dollars would have to be spent changing the equipment and assembly lines. In addition, both car dealers and manufacturers depend heavily on the sale of used cars for income. Such a revolutionary model as the Dymaxion would make old cars obsolete and depress all other sales. No manufacturer would attempt its production, especially in a Depression when each one was barely able to keep his business going.

There are those who have said to Bucky, "I'm very sorry your car was not a success."

"Why, what do you mean?" asks Bucky.

"Well, they didn't make it and you didn't make any money."

Bucky shakes his head. He wasn't trying to make any money. He was testing out a very special vehicle, the prototype of a "road-plane," and by every standard it was, in fact, a success.

Some of the new ideas which Bucky used in his Dymaxion have become standard equipment in today's cars. Perhaps, as parking space becomes increasingly scarce, as gasoline prices soar, the world will take another look at the Dymaxion's design.

9　　　Once again, Bucky was flat broke. His "success-
　　　ful" Dymaxion had taken everything he owned.
　　　Even his share in the ownership of Bear Island went to
pay debts. But the Dymaxion also had earned him a wide-
spread reputation in engineering circles. The Phelps Dodge
Corporation, an industrial group dealing in metal products,
offered him a job in the department of research. In this department, everyone's full-time work was exploring ideas and producing new products. If Bucky had to work at a regular nine-to-five
job, this one was certainly suited to his talents.

Mornings, Bucky and Allegra would leave the apartment on
88th Street. Bucky would head for downtown Manhattan.
Lucky Allegra had only to walk around the block to school, for
her father had planned it that way. Bucky did not want Allegra's
natural curiosity and abilities squashed by traditional ways of
learning. Why should every child in a classroom have to learn
the geography of Venezuela at exactly the same hour of a day?
So when the Fullers moved back to New York, they rented a
place around the corner from the Dalton School where the
teachers used new and different ways to teach children. (Some
years later, Aunt Rosy, too, was at the Dalton School working in
the office.)

At Phelps Dodge, Bucky used metals in new ways to solve
old problems. He designed a new type of brake drum. Made of
solid bronze, it eliminated the worrisome problem of "grab"
and "fade" in ordinary brakes. The inventive way in which he
used metals then made possible the disc brakes used on heavy
bombers today.

Fuller also persuaded the company to produce a new version
of the Dymaxion bathroom. His whole bathroom—completely
finished and furnished—weighed less than an ordinary bathtub
alone. During 1937 and 1938, twelve models rolled off the assembly line. Two of them went out to the Long Island house
of a friend, Christopher Morley.

Bucky, as usual, found dramatic ways to draw attention to his work. According to one friend, he placed the complete bathroom on an open flat-bed truck and drove it out to Long Island. Besides the bathroom, the truck carried a load of Hewletts, his in-laws. While Bucky drove slowly through quiet village streets, the assorted Hewletts flung streaming rolls of toilet paper from the truck. Few people who saw that parade could forget the Dymaxion Bathroom.

Twenty-five years later, more than half of these models were in "as-good-as-new" condition. Despite the bathroom's merits, Phelps Dodge decided not to produce any more models. Too many of their customers, too many plumbers were afraid of this new-style bathroom. One way or another, they thought it would cut into their business. Bucky was satisfied that he had proven his point. It was possible to mass-produce lightweight complete bathrooms that could be installed anywhere quickly.

Accustomed to working twenty hours a day, Bucky had more than enough time and energy to spare for his own projects. He tackled the job of arranging his beliefs, knowledge, and experience in an orderly fashion on paper.

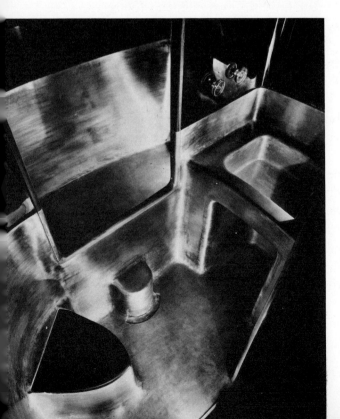

The first Phelps Dodge Dymaxion bathroom, 1937

To the world at large, Bucky Fuller seemed a brilliant, odd thinker who produced unconnected ideas and inventions: houses on poles, articles on pollution and energy, flying cars. Underneath those seemingly scattered ideas, however, was a constructive large-scale pattern. All of his efforts had been and were directed toward that resolution he had made years ago by the lake shore in Chicago: finding ways to do "more with less" so that more people everywhere can have more of everything. By weaving his thoughts into a book, Bucky hoped to show people that pattern.

Fuller titled the book *Nine Chains to the Moon.* In the introduction, he pointed out:

> If . . . all the people of the world were to stand upon one another's shoulders, they would make nine complete chains between the earth and the moon. If it is not so far to the moon, then it is not so far to the limits,—whatever, whenever or wherever they may be.

Bucky's friend, Christopher Morley, was a famous author and he persuaded his publisher to take Fuller's manuscript. When Bucky opened a letter from the publisher later, however, he had a rude shock.

"With regret," the publisher said it would be "an act of fraud" to publish Bucky's manuscript.

One part of Bucky's book dealt with the famous scientist Albert Einstein and his work. Bucky not only explained Einstein's ideas but also claimed that there could be practical applications of these to real life. At that time, Einstein's theories were considered so difficult that supposedly only ten people in the whole world understood them. Looking at that list, the publishers had not found Bucky's name on it.

Dismayed, Bucky shook himself into action. He wrote the publisher: Einstein was then living in Princeton, New Jersey. Why not send the manuscript to *him* and ask *him* if the work was satisfactory?

Months passed. Bucky heard nothing more from the publisher. When the phone finally did ring, it was a Dr. Fishbein who was calling. Fishbein's friend, Dr. Einstein, planned to spend that weekend in New York City. If Bucky was free Sunday evening, Dr. Einstein wanted to discuss the manuscript with him. Could Bucky come to the Riverside Drive apartment of the Fishbeins to meet Einstein?

"If Bucky was free . . . !"

For a meeting such as this with the world's greatest scientific thinker, Bucky would do anything and everything to be sure that he was free.

Surrounded by people in that high-ceilinged apartment, Dr. Albert Einstein looked even smaller than he was. As Bucky came forward to be introduced, he was impressed by the man's air of gentle goodness. Einstein rose promptly and led Bucky into Fishbein's study where the two could talk privately. In the study, Bucky saw his manuscript lying on a table.

"Young man," began Dr. Einstein.

What would he say about Bucky's explanations and writings? Would he criticize, condemn, or scold him for his boldness?

"I've been over your book and am notifying your publisher that I am pleased and satisfied with your explanation," said Dr. Einstein.

He added that Bucky had in fact amazed him. Einstein had never thought that his work could have any practical applications. Rather, he thought that his theories might simply help scientists to a better understanding of the Universe.

Years later, scientists applying Einstein's formula unlocked the secret of atomic energy and developed the most devastating bomb known to mankind. Bucky thought often of the pain that the peace-loving Einstein must have felt at this use of his work.

When Bucky left that study, every word that Einstein had uttered was carved into his memory. It mattered little to Bucky that the world called him a "charming nut" or "crackpot," for he had had a unique and unforgettable satisfaction. The world-famous Nobel Prize winner had not only approved of what Bucky had written but also credited him with adding to man's understanding of the Universe.

When *Nine Chains to the Moon* was published in 1938, *Newsweek* magazine said: ". . . a dream book of the future . . . this ruddy-faced, gray-haired inventor is no nut. Great stuff!" But few people bought it then. It was to be a book of and for the future.

When Phelps Dodge asked Bucky to forecast the future use of copper, he looked naturally to the past. Huge amounts of copper had been mined for use in World War I. Bucky knew that metals are not eaten up like strawberries; nor do they disappear forever. Rather, they are melted down and come back on the market as scrap. Looking for patterns, Bucky discovered the cycle for recirculating copper occurred every twenty-two and a half years.

Three years after his study, Bucky answered the phone and heard the voice of the research director at Phelps Dodge.

"Bucky, it's happened."

Just as Bucky had predicted, the copper producers of America found themselves in 1939 drowning in a flood of copper scrap. They had neither expected nor wanted this flood. Greater profits came from mining new copper than from using copper scrap. (The unfortunate result was that they sold the scrap to German and Japanese companies. Within a year this scrap was being used for weapons against America in World War II.)

By then, Bucky was working for *Fortune* magazine where he continued to map trends and patterns for readers. He invented or worked out a unit of measurement which he called "energy slaves." With these energy slaves for measuring, he could show how much power was available to serve the people of each country. His World Energy Map published in the tenth anniversary issue of *Fortune* in February 1940 made clear the terrible gap between the "haves" and the "have-nots." As late as 1950, the half-century mark, Asians still had only 2 energy slaves per person, while North Americans had 347 such units to serve each person's needs.

Although he did not write many articles himself, Bucky was a valuable resource for the magazine. He had more ideas than he could explore in two lifetimes and was generous in sharing them. The other editors picked his brain for ideas like people collecting the produce from a flourishing vegetable garden.

One design that he whipped up in that period was the Mechanical Wing. The Wing, containing a kitchen, energy unit, and bathroom, could be carried easily on Fuller's A-frame trailer to any campsite or vacation home. Although the Wing was never manufactured, millions of boat owners today use the A-frame trailer to haul their boats from home to lakes and rivers.

This drawing of Fuller's Mechanical Wing appeared in The Architectural Forum, *October 1940*

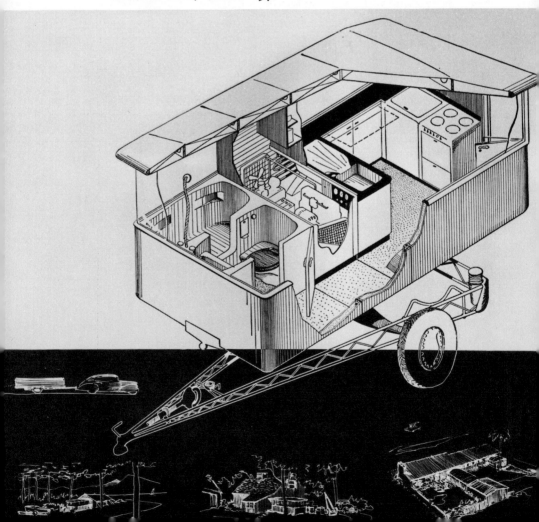

Not all of Bucky's ideas were geared to a far-off future. In 1940, he took a summer vacation trip with Christopher Morley. Driving through Missouri, the two men passed field after field of waving wheat. The wheat fields shimmered under the hot sun. Suddenly, Bucky's eyes lit on a row of steel grain bins. Pointing to the glistening cylinders, he developed an idea that was both practical and immediately useful.

A cylinder encloses more space than a cube of the same wall area. The grain bin, a most efficient form of engineering, could be a unit for housing—fireproof and much cheaper than anything on the market. Steel cylinders for housing could be as easily produced in a factory as the grain bins were.

At the end of his explanations, Bucky shrugged his shoulders. As always, he had no money to carry out the idea. Morley, caught by Bucky's enthusiasm, made a proposal. He had just written a novel called *Kitty Foyle*. If the book became a best seller, he'd use some of the money to back Bucky's idea.

Kitty Foyle was a smashing success. So Fuller redesigned the grain bins for living purposes and took his plans to the company which made the original bins.

Like the Dymaxion House, the Dymaxion Deployment Unit (his name for the bin) was built from the top down. The roof, which Fuller designed with curved joints, was assembled on the ground first and then hoisted up. The body sheets, too, were put together on the ground and then raised to join with the roof. With this method, no scaffold was necessary to build the shelter.

The first unit was assembled on the testing grounds of the Butler Company in Kansas City. The president of the company as well as the engineers came to inspect the Dymaxion Deployment Unit. That day the temperature was one hundred degrees in the shade. Sitting out under the noon sun, the metal walls of the building had become scorching hot. When the president wanted to go inside, the engineers shook their heads and advised him not to go in.

"You'll burn up," one of them predicted.

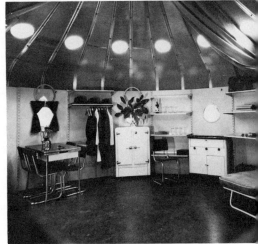

Above: the exterior of a Dymaxion Deployment Unit; below: two views of the interior of a D.D.U.

A stubborn man, the president insisted on entering the unit. A minute later, he called out:

"Hey, it's air-conditioned in here."

Although the others thought he was joking, they followed him in. To the amazement of all, it *was* cool inside. How could it be? There was no machinery for air conditioning in that building. When the men lit cigarettes, the smoke patterns told them that a cold down-draft was operating inside.

Long ago, Fuller had worked on the idea that there were purely "local" patterns in the movements of air, energy, and heat levels. One local pattern is the Gulf Stream, whose waters are much warmer than the surrounding ocean waters.

Everyone knows that hot air rises. Just so, the hot air surrounding the outside of the cylinder rose in a column. Through little openings around the base, stale air from inside rushed out to join the rising air. The pressure inside dropped. Cooler air was sucked down through the center of the column to fill the vacuum. By providing the right shape and venting controls (top and bottom), Bucky cleverly took advantage of a natural pattern. The hotter the sun shone, the cooler it was inside. He had created "sun-powered air conditioning."

The D.D.U. was born in time to fill a pressing need. In September of 1939, German armies had invaded Poland. Almost all of Europe plunged into the most terrible war in history. Great Britain looked across the Atlantic to the United States for support.

"Give us the tools and we will finish the job," promised Winston Churchill, Britain's Prime Minister.

Sympathetic America responded. President Roosevelt declared that America must become the "arsenal of democracy." Tanks, trucks, planes, and D.D.U.s rolled off the production lines. Lightweight, easily assembled, the D.D.U. could be flown to any part of the world where shelter was urgently needed.

Each D.D.U. package included a tool kit with the tools commonly used by carpenters and mechanics. Some officials had objected to including the tools. They argued that the kits would be stolen as soon as the units were assembled.

"That's what I expect, too," Fuller answered.

Yet he insisted that the kits be included. He figured that the workers would put up the buildings in a hurry so that they could make off with the tools. It was a cheap way to get people to build the units quickly. It worked.

Hundreds of D.D.U.s serving as radar shacks dotted remote corners of the world. On the Persian Gulf, they served as dormitories for the mechanics and airmen who were assembling and transferring planes to the Allies. As the President had said, this was an "emergency as serious as war itself."

While American eyes and hands were turned toward helping Europe, the flash came from Hawaii:

"Enemy air raid—not a drill."

The Empire of Japan had attacked Pearl Harbor. By the end of that day, December 7, 1941, more than two thousand servicemen were dead.

Angry and determined, America's energies turned toward defending herself. No more D.D.U.s were produced. Every bit of steel and metal was necessary for the actual weapons of war. Manufacturing guns, tanks, and airplanes ranked at the top of the list now, and shelter ranked low. Armies—if they stopped at all —would take cover in trenches and tents.

10   In the first sixteen days after the attack on Pearl Harbor, the railroads moved 600,000 troops across the country. Change and movement were in the air for everyone. Men and women went into the armed forces to fight, into defense plants to build weapons of war.

Bucky Fuller, too, put aside his peacetime job to take one that helped the war effort. Moving to Washington, D.C., he became the director of the mechanical engineering section of the Board of Economic Warfare. Anne remained in New York until Allegra finished her school year at Dalton.

Now Bucky Fuller made another one of his surprising decisions. In a time and a town where overworked, anxious people turned to cocktail parties to relieve pressures, fun-loving Bucky stopped drinking completely. He also stopped smoking, and has done neither since.

"The war was something serious," explains Bucky.

He had found too that if he was drinking, people tended to write off his talk about the design revolution as drunken gibberish. Despite his decision, Bucky still was greeted at planning meetings with such remarks as: "We don't want any of that house-by-air nonsense." And everyone at the meeting would laugh.

An old proverb says: He who laughs last laughs best. Eleven years later, this "house-by-air nonsense" made front page news in the *New York Times*. The Marine Corps demonstrated delivery by air of a Fuller-designed shelter. Hailing it as the beginning of a new era in shelter, the *Times* editorial praised the domed haven that would keep a platoon of men "from freezing their noses and toes, keep them dry and human. . . ."

Those early days of the war were anxious ones, filled with news of defeats and deaths. New words entered every American's vocabulary: radar, bazooka guns, Molotov cocktail. Zippers disappeared; the metal went into weapons. Silk stockings disappeared; the material went into parachutes. People worked at two jobs or long hours of overtime, tumbling exhausted into bed in the early hours of the morning. For energetic Bucky, such a fast pace of doubled-up work was simply normal.

Allegra and Bucky in Washington, D.C., 1944

His home life, too, became normal when Anne and Allegra joined him in Washington. Allegra may have missed seeing Aunt Rosy's familiar face in the Dalton School office, for she was enrolled now in the Madeira School. At fifteen, Allegra seemed to be a blend of both sides of the family. Short and sturdy like Bucky, she carried herself very straight and moved gracefully. She had something of Anne's personality, too. Sensitive to the feelings of others, she was a tactful girl who did not like to gossip. Anne and Bucky could be proud of their bright, graceful daughter.

They had something more to celebrate in 1942. Years ago, Bucky's mother had warned Monroe Hewlett that Bucky would make an "irresponsible" son-in-law. Yet a quarter of a century later, Bucky and Anne were still together, marking and enjoying their silver wedding anniversary.

Through all those years, Bucky had continued to search for the single system that Nature used to build her structures. In his Navy days, he had been much impressed by vectors, those lines that mapped forces or energies. A vector had definite length. It didn't go on absurdly forever to the nowhere of infinity. As he investigated the mathematical behavior of these energy events, Fuller felt that he was on the right track. In those days, it was just a hunch. He needed still to work out the supporting network of arithmetic and geometry.

For more than twenty years Bucky had studied, learned, and explored. Many of the facts that he rediscovered in his experiments had been long known in mathematics. But the questions that Bucky asked after making his discoveries led him into new directions. He had discussed his work with Homer Le Sourd, formerly at Milton Academy and then a teacher of mathematics at Harvard. Much to the two men's surprise, they found that Bucky had traveled far afield from the known and usual concepts in mathematics.

"Should I go on with it?" a questioning Bucky said to Le Sourd.

Le Sourd hesitated. He could not answer one way or the other. There was nothing in Bucky's work that wasn't logical or that was contradicted by the work of others. Certainly, his was "elegant" work. But Le Sourd could not then see where these explorations had significance or what their final meaning might be.

As usual, Bucky settled that question by asking himself still another question.

"Could Nature have developed this entrancing cul-de-sac [or blind alley] just for *me?*" Bucky asked himself. "No," he decided. "I can't be *that* important!"

So, late at night and into the early morning hours, Bucky scribbled and experimented with an unshakable optimism. Bucky at work was an energy happening in himself. His short, thinning, white hair bristled, his dark eyebrows climbed high, his hand with the pencil flew over the paper. When Bucky put down his pencil, he turned often to a huge pile of ping-pong balls in a corner of the room.

What did ping-pong balls have to do with mapping energy and Nature's geometry?

They were Bucky's building blocks as he attempted to build a model of the energy lines in Nature.

Starting with one ball as a center, Bucky packed a layer of as many others as he could possibly fit around this one (figure 1). Carefully, he built up more layers (figure 2). He saw that the outline of all these ping-pong balls formed a polyhedron (figure 3). His fourteen-sided figure had faces of six equal squares and eight equal triangles. Each triangle touched four squares, each square touched four triangles. All edges were equal in length. No matter how many layers he added he always got this same many-sided figure.

Now he settled down to mapping the vectors of his poly-hedron: those lines of force which had a direction and a length that could be measured. Remembering the way a part of a hoop works to hold a barrel stave in place, Bucky imagined a similar band sweeping around the outside of his figure. The force vector along each edge equaled the force vector from the center of the polyhedron to the corners of each square or triangle. That is to say, the distance from the center of the polyhedron to the corner of each square or triangle was the same as the length of each side of those shapes. All the lines of force equalized one another. He called this beautifully balanced figure a Vector Equilibrium (figure 4).

What would happen if he took out the center ball?

The balls shifted and formed now an icosahedron or twenty-sided figure. By removing still more balls from the center, the figure shrank down to an octahedron (eight sides). A count showed that there were six balls making up this octahedron. Finally, he reduced his ping-pong balls to the simplest solid form

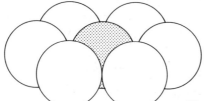

Figure 1

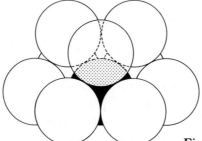

Figure 2

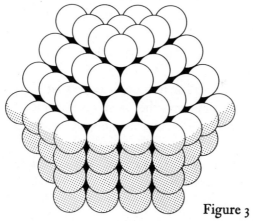

Figure 3

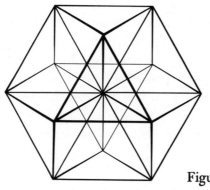

Figure 4

that could stand by itself. He got a tetrahedron, a pyramid with three sides plus its base. The tetrahedron consisted of four balls.

The South Sea islander piling his coconuts and the fruit dealer piling up his oranges for display had practiced this "closest packing of spheres," but few scientists had investigated or paid attention to this nest of tetrahedrons.

Nature, Bucky knew, uses certain geometric shapes over and over to build her structures. These basic shapes are like the letters of her special alphabet. Combining them in different ways, she makes the words—or more elaborate forms—of the environment. Circles are found in the shapes of flowers, berries, planets. Triangles make the shape of insect wings, crystals, bats.

Now Bucky drew some conclusions from his experiments and formulas. Nature always chooses the most economical method to build her structures. In reducing the ping-pong balls, he had demonstrated that the stable or rigid tetrahedron represented the shortest, most economical energy network. This remarkable figure was the smallest possible "system" that could be identified.

Going one step further, he decided that all of Nature's building and patterning must be based on this one. *Any and all other shapes found in Nature are simply different forms of the tetrahedron.* Put simply, the tetrahedron then was Nature's first basic event. It might be described as something like a least common denominator, one from which she started her structuring.

Slowly, from this discovery, he began developing a system of mathematics describing the lines of force that occur in atoms, molecules, and crystals. It took many years and more discoveries to convince others.

What pleased Bucky most was that in mapping lines of force and energies, he had been able to make a visible, touchable model. A century ago, scientists dealing with energy felt that they were dealing with something invisible, something that could not be explained or demonstrated with models. They used algebraic formulas to express for themselves the relationships of energy. Without models, the rest of the world could no longer

Drawings made almost a century ago from microscopic studies of marine protozoa show shapes based on the tetrahedron, the octahedron, or the icosahedron

see, touch, or understand scientists' work. (Using paper, rope, ping-pong balls, Bucky continually "models" his ideas to make them understood in public lectures.)

Fuller's work suggests that this gap need never have existed. From the earliest Greek thinkers on, those who accepted the static geometry of lines and points had been using the wrong model, the cube. If you make a cube with little sticks and rubber joints, the cube always collapses. No wonder then that scientists could not make models of energy events.

Although his system of Energetic Geometry was by no means completed, Bucky found an immediate practical use for his triangles and arithmetic.

Years before, while flying in Astor's plane, Bucky had sensed the need for a new kind of map. How can any flat map show an exact picture of a round world? he wondered. To show some areas accurately, others must be distorted. A commonly used map, the Mercator, is very accurate in the center, at the equator. But as you move away from the equator toward the North or South poles, lands and distances get stretched out of their true shape and size. Greenland appears six times bigger than it really is. At the North Pole, points that measure one mile apart show up as being thousands of miles apart. In many maps, the tops of the continents don't join together; Antarctica is totally missing.

Even on a world globe, you cannot see the whole at one time. You can read only a part of the globe and then must spin it around to see the rest of the world. And, of course, airplane pilots cannot carry a globe very conveniently with them. Bucky, who always liked to look at "wholes," could not accept such incomplete, distorted tools.

Now, he used neat, stark, and very accurate mathematics to carve up the globe into perfect triangles. He transferred these triangle systems to the equal triangles of his Vector Equilibrium, or polyhedron. Then, just like taking the skin off an animal, Bucky unpeeled the skin of this solid polyhedron to produce a single, continuous surface. To flatten out the skin, he had to make cuts or "sinuses" around the outside edges. He called this flattened-out globe skin the Dymaxion Map.

Fuller's "Dymaxion Airocean World" map.
Copyright 1954 by R. Buckminster Fuller.
U.S. Pat. 2,939,676

What had he achieved?

He had taken all the information off the world globe and made it accurately available in a flat map. Europe and Asia were no longer split in two. Since all the cuts or sinuses occurred in the oceans, the continents for the first time were shown linked together without breaks in their outlines.

In Bucky's map, the chain of continents appears as a single island in a single ocean, a fact well known, perhaps, but not easily seen before. No one area of distance is more distorted than another.

There is no "right side up" in Bucky's map. The perfect triangles can be cut out and assembled in many different ways. In one assembly, you see the world as it looks from the North Pole. Putting them together in still another way, you see the world as it looks from the tip of South America. All kinds of geographic facts suddenly show on Bucky's map with a new and dramatic sharpness.

Most people think that the world always gets colder as you go north. Using the spectrum of color to chart the coldest and hottest spots, the Dymaxion Map points out a contrary fact. Europe gets colder as you head east. (Napoleon could have profited from Bucky's map when he invaded Russia in 1812. His plans did not take into account the relentless cold which bogged down his army and finally defeated him.)

Encyclopedias had said no flat map projection could keep the proportion true, while the U.S. Patent Office declared that all the possible mathematics of projections or map-making had been exhausted in 1900. Some mathematicians pooh-poohed Fuller's method and figures, calling them "pure invention."

Bucky turned these criticisms to his advantage. If, indeed, these were pure invention, then he argued that his invention deserved a patent. Finally, the Patent Office agreed with him and granted Bucky a patent, the first ever given for a method of projection.

In early March of 1943, two exciting and happy events took place. One was the wedding of Rosy, Bucky's sister, to a naval officer, Alphonse Kenison, who shared her interests and her love of boats. The other was the Dymaxion Map's public appearance in *Life* magazine.

More people bought that issue of *Life* than any other in its history. Professors from Harvard and Princeton wrote, praising *Life* for making the map available. Thousands of Americans, following directions, used a glue pot, scissors, and patience to cut out and "marry the segments of Buckminster Fuller's world" into a solid polyhedron. One very funny letter writer gave "Orchids to *Life* and Mr. Fuller . . . for keeping Americans at home" that weekend. By staying home to work on the map, he pointed out, Americans had saved thousands of gallons of precious gasoline.

Gasoline, sugar, meat—all kinds of goods were rationed now. Every family could buy only a limited amount each week. America was helping to feed, clothe, and arm almost all the free world as well as its own citizens. By the end of 1942, the factories had turned out 48,000 military planes, 56,000 combat vehicles, and 670,000 machine guns.

Wichita, Kansas, had become a center for producing bombers, and the population there doubled in one week from 100,000 to 200,000. Workers in the Wichita plants led a miserable crowded life. Up to three people shared a single room and used the beds in eight-hour shifts around the clock. Wichita workers had still another worry to trouble them: Would there be jobs for them in the airplane industry after the war ended?

Few could see the need for any great numbers of planes in the postwar world. Many quit to look for jobs where there might be a more secure future. In fact, more people were quitting each week than were hired.

What would persuade workers to stay on the job? How could this alarming trend which threatened production be reversed? Someone in Washington remembered Buckminster Fuller's talk about mass production of houses. Perhaps workers might stay if they thought the aircraft industry could convert later to producing houses.

Labor leaders visited Bucky to explore with him this idea. Bucky was confident that it could be done. There was really no great difference between making parts for his Dymaxion House and parts for B-29 bombers. The labor leaders asked Bucky to fly to Kansas where the president of Beech Aircraft made a deal with him: The company would lend him space, engineers, and workers to develop his plans.

Bucky promptly resigned from his government job and moved to Kansas. There the industry was buzzing with news of Fuller's house project, and he was invited to speak with workers at all fourteen companies in the Wichita area.

Suddenly the worried government officials studying those alarming charts spotted an unbelievable change. In a few short weeks after Bucky's talks, the trend of workers quitting had reversed itself completely. The industry was both keeping its employees on the job and gaining new ones steadily. There was no question about it. The credit for this upward swing belonged to R. Buckminster Fuller.

Drawing up new plans for what became the Wichita House, Bucky blended in parts of his earlier Dymaxions, the 4D House, and the Deployment Unit. This house, too, hung from a mast and was supported by cables which anchored it to the ground. In outline, the circular house with its cone-shaped roof looked somewhat like a turnip. The house weighed three tons, just what Bucky had estimated in 1927. (Most houses that size weighed one hundred and fifty tons.) Yet no one piece by itself weighed more than ten pounds. A man could lift or hold a piece in one hand while his other hand was free to fasten or bolt the piece in place. All the parts could be packed into a crate on a conveyer belt, the lid nailed down, and the whole house shipped anywhere in the United States at a shipping cost of less than $100.

With an order from the Air Force in his pocket, Bucky started production on two prototypes. He designed new dies to stamp out the gleaming aluminum sheets that would become the walls of the house. Now, side by side, the assembly lines were turning out airplane parts and Wichita House parts.

The war ended in August of 1945. Less than two months later, the completed Wichita House was opened for viewing. People hungry for new housing came in droves to see it. Outside, the aluminum walls seemed to match the sky; the curving plexiglass windows caught and reflected the sun. On top of the roof, a tall ventilator on ball bearings provided both air conditioning and safety. When Kansas tornadoes blew, the ventilator lifted like the safety valve on a boiler to equalize air pressures and keep the house from being blown apart.

Inside, the domed ceiling soared to sixteen feet, creating a sense of space and luxury. Practical as always, Bucky had simplified the housekeeping chores. Motor-driven revolving shelves put everything within quick, easy reach of the housekeeper. Women estimated that they could clean the whole house in half an hour.

The Dymaxion Dwelling Machine (Wichita House)

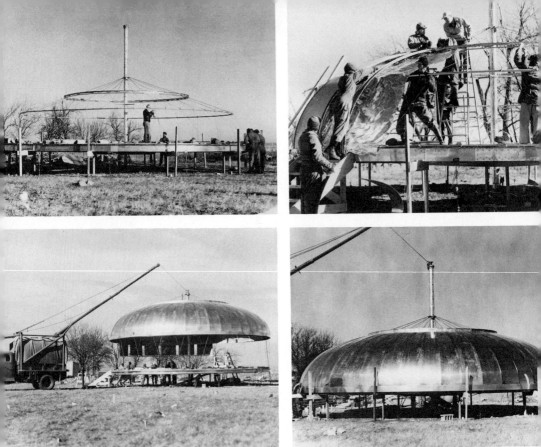

Steps in the assembly of the Wichita House

Beech Aircraft, figuring costs and allowing for profit, settled on a price of $6,500 for the house.

"I'll buy it," was the immediate enthusiastic response of the public. Over thirty-seven thousand letters (many with checks) came pouring in to prove it.

All signs pointed to a smash success. The demand for housing was great. People had money from wartime jobs and couldn't wait to spend it. Here was a product that promised to make millions of dollars for its backers. Because Beech Aircraft had chosen to stay in the airplane business, a new company was formed. Ten million dollars had to be raised to start this exciting new industry. Shares of stock were sold and resold.

In all this excitement, enthusiasm, and cheerful expectation of riches, one person smiled less and less often. Bucky Fuller was shaking his head.

"It's premature," he declared. Too soon, too early for this new industry to get off the ground. Making a single house for an exhibit did not mean that the conditions or tools were ready for making thousands of houses.

To deliver and assemble houses on the sites, a very special kind of truck was needed, one with a great boom attached to it. There were no such trucks. Nor was there any network of dealers to sell and distribute the houses. Even if the houses could be delivered, the building industry could not agree on who should install them. Already the unions were squabbling among themselves as to who should hook up which part.

Bucky and his backers could not agree. The backers wanted to gamble that the very real problems could be solved. Bucky's conscience would not let him continue. He could not bring himself to sell people something that could not be delivered.

Who was right, Bucky or the backers? Could the problems have been overcome?

No one will ever know. For R. Buckminster Fuller reluctantly but firmly shut down the whole effort. Fuller Houses, Inc., died as quickly as it had been born. Furious stockholders denounced Bucky as a bungler. Bucky Fuller had turned his back on a fortune and the world turned its back on him. The leading business magazine of the time announced that Buckminster Fuller was all washed up.

Total parts for a Wichita House; no single part weighs more than ten pounds

11 One of Bucky's beliefs is that what is going on at the moment is not really what is important or counts in Nature's game plan. For a honey bee, chasing the nectar is what's important; for Nature, the important happening is the cross-pollination of plants that occurs. Bucky Fuller was chasing bigger things than the "honey" that the Wichita House might have brought. The Wichita House project had been a detour. Along the way, he had caught a glimpse of something else to be explored in his developing mathematics. With enough time, he thought that he could pin it down.

Meanwhile it was summer, and time to enjoy the first glimpse of Bear Island as it came into sight. Thanks to sister Rosy, who loved the place passionately, no outsiders owned any part of the island now. Scraping together all her money, Rosy had bought back the shares which had gone to Bucky's creditors for the Dymaxion Car. Over the years, a grateful Bucky had managed to pay her back.

Now the boat nosed into the harbor toward Hardie's headland and he could see the ledge on the right. He craned his head to look and the broad grin grew even broader. Yes, just as he had expected, there was a fish hawk's nest on the ledge as there had been every year.

The summer before, Bucky had set up some tricky walkways in the ice pond. Painting the kitchen, teaching Allegra to sail, fixing gutters. . . . There was always more than enough to fill the days at Bear Island. At night, after supper, he wrote up columns of happenings on the island. When people came down to breakfast, each found a copy of this morning newspaper neatly folded by the plate.

Throughout the vacation and afterward, Bucky reviewed his situation. What had he accomplished so far in fifty years of living? Should he continue in his work which he called "comprehensive anticipatory design science"? Was the world right in declaring him a failure?

Yet Bucky Fuller had evidence that some of his hunches were correct. War needs and improved instruments had begun washing out the lines that separated the sciences. The new sciences emerging, like biochemistry and biophysics, supported his argument. To understand the Universe, it was necessary to study the whole system rather than specialize in one department of study. A small but increasing number of scientists had begun to agree with him.

In Washington, Bucky had discussed his work with the scientists who met for lunch at the Cosmos Club. Thornton Wilder, a playwright and also an excellent mathematician, urged Bucky to copyright his ideas before someone else took credit for them. Wilder felt that Bucky was uncovering some of the most important principles since Isaac Newton had discovered gravity. Additionally, every one of his prototypes had worked, and worked very well indeed. All this gave Bucky confidence.

Once again Bucky Fuller came to an important decision. With the little money that he had saved in the war years, he would buy time. No more detours into other work. From now on, he would concentrate on developing his geometry of energy.

The apartment in Forest Hills, New York, became his laboratory, study, and workshop. There was scarcely space left over in the little three-room apartment for the purposes of living. Diagrams, figures, formulas—Bucky scribbled constantly. He would wake up in the night, sit up, and work for hours. He wrote on the backs of envelopes, napkins, any piece of paper that was at hand. For this project, he knew his figures had to be absolutely accurate. Using spherical trigonometry, he worked for two years.

Although Bucky worked steadily, he did not cut himself off from the world this time. Whenever and wherever he was invited to talk, he accepted.

At Dartmouth College in 1947, the program chairman mentioned that R. Buckminster Fuller had been a guest speaker there many years ago. With a gleam in his eye, Bucky stood up to begin his lecture. His voice went in fits and starts, like an engine revving up slowly. The audience listened attentively to Bucky as he went through his thinking-out-loud process.

Over the past seventeen years, he had consumed and processed tons and tons of food, air, and water. His body had long since shed the skin, nail, and hair cells that had been Bucky Fuller in 1930. Even the hall where he had spoken before had disappeared in a fire. Possibly, he concluded, the only part of him that had been on the Dartmouth campus before was his glasses.

A laughing, delighted audience leaned forward to hear more from this man who produced one startling idea after another. Young people in particular always responded warmly to Bucky's ideas and his way of putting them across.

As a guest lecturer in the 1948 Summer Institute of Black Mountain College in North Carolina, Bucky got room, board, and a tiny salary. Better than money, though, was the bonus of eager students willing to listen and work with him. Together they made strange-looking models of spheres and half spheres. The models were strange-looking because their rounded surfaces were networks of triangles. Bucky was testing an idea that had occurred to him while working on his Dymaxion Map.

Bucky and students in 1948

If he could develop a three-way great circle grid or network
. . . If he could divide his triangles into smaller and smaller ones
. . . If he could do the geometry properly . . . Why, then the
dome would behave in an extraordinary way. He should end up
with the strongest, lightest, and most efficient means of enclosing space ever made by man. *If* he did the geometry accurately.

By early 1949, Bucky was satisfied with his calculations. The
time had come to build real domes, big ones that would prove
his theories and demonstrate this quality of super-strength. Only
one problem remained, the same one that he always bumped up
against. Money. Where could he go for money? The business
world had dismissed Bucky as a fool about money and a failure. Bucky himself, burned by the Wichita House disaster, had
no wish to put his project at the mercy of outside backers. Still,
he needed money. Around and around Bucky's thoughts went
and finally, as always, he shared them with Anne.

He needed money to buy materials, the best possible materials
for his prototypes. But who besides Bucky could believe in a
structure whose strength depended on the mind and geometry
of one man?

Cutting through to the heart of the matter, Anne asked a
practical question. How much money? Then she pointed out
that he could "go" to her for the money. Her latest legacy included valuable shares of stock. Since she had always had confidence in Bucky, she willingly sold the shares. It was just enough
to make the difference.

A cheerful, confident Bucky drove south to Black Mountain College. Students from the Chicago Institute of Design
joined him there to work on the summer's project, setting up a
fourteen-foot hemisphere. When spread out on the ground, the
makings of the dome looked like the pieces of a giant Tinkertoy.
Aluminum aircraft tubing with cables laced through made up
the dozens of triangles.

Almost everybody at the Institute turned out to watch it
go up. Some must have let their breaths out in a sigh of relief. It
went up and stayed up. Now to test its strength.

Bucky and students test a geodesic dome at Black Mountain College in 1949

Standing under the dome, nine men grabbed at the joints of the triangles. Then, swinging their feet clear from the ground, they hung like monkeys from the dome. That spidery, fragile-looking network of tubes and cables stood fast. No dimpling, no caving in. All the forces, inside and outside, pushing and pulling, were perfectly balanced to provide the greatest possible strength.

Bucky Fuller had successfully used Nature's basic event, the tetrahedron, to make his spherical framework. The edges of the tetrahedrons joined to make great circle arcs. In mathematics, the shortest distance between two points on a sphere is called a geodesic. Consequently, Bucky named his structure a geodesic dome.

Another practical application of his mathematics, one of alternating tetrahedrons and octahedrons, he called the Octet truss. This truss can carry enormous loads. Even Bucky was surprised by the performance of his Octet truss. An aluminum one weighing only sixty-five pounds supported a load of six tons, or the equal of a small Army tank.

His Octet truss demonstrated the meaning of synergy, one of Bucky's favorite words. By his definition, synergy is the only word in our language meaning the behavior of wholes unpredicted by behavior of their parts.

To illustrate, he asks audiences to consider the metals of chrome, nickel, and iron. Each one has a certain pulling strength. Combine these together into the alloy chrome-nickel steel. Adding the strengths of these metals together, you would expect the new alloy to have a strength of 260,000 pounds per square inch, or the sum of its parts. But, in fact, you get a surprise: The alloy has a pulling strength of 350,000 pounds per square inch, or a "whole" that is greater than the strength of all its linked parts added together. Synergy plays a key part in Bucky's Synergetic-Energetic Geometry.

Bucky traveled from college to college and his lectures stimulated students to build bigger and bigger domes. Under his direction, the students' domes demonstrated another valuable quality. Because his dome's strength lies in the invisible mathematics, it

Drawing of an Octet truss

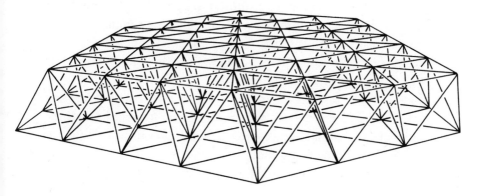

could be made of almost any material. Wood, plastic, aluminum —even cardboard—worked. And it used less material to cover more space than any building ever seen.

Cornell students built a geodesic Miniature Earth. Standing inside this geodesic earth dome, you could see through the open network of struts to the heavens above. It was as if you had taken an elevator to the center of the earth and had x-ray eyes to look up, around, and out. The eye could trace a bronze screen overlay of the continents. Its North-South Pole axis paralleled the earth's axis and all the real stars in the heavens appeared in true zenith over the Miniature Earth just as they did over the real earth. In this strikingly effective planetarium, Fuller says you could "see and feel the earth to be revolving in the presence of the stars."

Although 90 percent of Americans had heard of those strange things called flying saucers, only a tiny fraction of a percent had heard of Fuller's domes. Even fewer thought that the domes had any value or could fill any real need. Many dismissed them as beautiful but useless objects, a novelty to be admired in the Pentagon Garden or the Museum of Modern Art. Fuller was undisturbed by those opinions. He invented and then waited until the world came around to needing what he invented.

In the case of the domes, the need appeared when the Ford Motor Company planned to celebrate its fiftieth anniversary in 1953. Next to the River Rouge plant in Michigan stood the Rotunda, a circular office building with a courtyard open to the sky. The first Henry Ford had often wished that the courtyard could be covered by a dome and used all year round. To mark the company's anniversary, his grandson, young Henry Ford, decided to cover the courtyard. He asked the leading architects and engineers for a design.

"No way," said the experts. A conventional dome of the size needed would weigh 160 tons. Such a weight would crush the walls of the Rotunda. Still, young Henry continued to hunt for a way to carry out his grandfather's wish.

If an ordinary dome could not be put on top, how about an

Miniature Earth at Cornell University, 1952

extraordinary one? Perhaps something like the domes that Buckminster Fuller demonstrated and lectured about?

"Yes," Bucky answered simply and without hesitation. It could be done.

"Only a fool or crackpot like Fuller would try," said the experts. Besides the engineering problems, there was an added problem of time. Ford wanted the dome finished in less than four months.

Bucky himself had no doubts. The two years that he had invested in those pages and pages of careful calculations were now ready to pay off. Once the calculations had been done, they could be used for any size dome that had the parts arranged in the same fashion.

Still, Bucky took no chances on this job. He used the Octet truss with more struts than were strictly necessary. Even so, the ninety-three-foot dome that he designed weighed just eight and a half tons. (A much larger dome designed later for the Ford Company weighed only a fraction of that first one.)

"Bucky Fuller Finds a Client," headlined the article in the architects' magazine. At last someone had come to Bucky to buy what he had designed. The customer found, too, that Bucky had locked up this formula which came straight from Nature. Five months after he celebrated his fifty-sixth birthday, Bucky had applied for a patent on his "framework for enclosing space." No one could build a geodesic dome without a license or permission from Fuller.

Once the contract was signed, the Ford Company moved quickly to manufacture the parts. Punches designed especially for this job made holes in the ends of the struts; workmen riveted the struts into small triangles and joined the small triangles to larger triangles. High over the open Rotunda court, a giant lacy web of struts began spreading out. Two days before the deadline in April, the last strut was riveted into place. Fuller had pulled it off; the impossible had been done. The Rotunda had been covered in record-breaking time at less cost than expected. Stockholders who came to the annual meeting found it beautiful as well.

Bucky, always quick with a rhyme, wrote a jingle to be sung to the tune of "Home on the Range." The last lines went:

> Just give me a home in a great circle dome
> Where the stresses and strains are at ease.

At right: A view from inside the Ford Rotunda dome

After the success of the Ford Company dome, the whole world seemed to take up Bucky's song. The Air Force, the Marines, the Department of Commerce all came shopping for the domes. Each order presented a different set of problems and requirements. Yet Bucky's domes satisfied each one's needs.

For the Marines, Fuller designed a small hut that could shelter six men. The shelters were so cheap that they could be used and then left behind when the troops moved out. The Marines nicknamed this paperboard container "the Kleenex House." More soberly, their leaders declared it the first major improvement in military shelter since the introduction of the tent over two thousand years ago. In different sizes, the domes replaced forty-seven different kinds of shelter that the Marines had been using.

"I personally can appreciate Fuller and his dome," wrote one grateful Marine pilot in a letter to *Time* magazine. The pilots landing on a barren island had had to fight winds and choking dirt. As if by magic, two huge hangar domes appeared shortly after to protect men and planes. Here was shelter delivered by air to remote parts of the globe, just as Bucky Fuller had predicted in 1927.

The Air Force planned a string of radar installations along the Arctic Circle to defend America against surprise attacks. Because of the extreme weather conditions in the Arctic, the Air Force asked Fuller for a structure that could be flown in pieces and put together in less than a day. The materials in such a structure had to stand up against winds of 210 miles an hour yet allow radar beams to pass through. (Structural steel, which reflects radar beams, could not be used.) Fuller more than met the requirements with a forty-foot-high fiberglass plastic dome. His "radome" went up in fourteen hours and withstood winds of 220 miles an hour. Hugging the northern edges of Canada and Alaska, the three-thousand-mile strip of radomes forms America's DEW (Distant Early Warning) line.

While he was working on such military projects, the armed services insisted that he be investigated.

"Why?" asked Bucky Fuller.

Because whatever he created for them would naturally become "top secret," he was told. Only those people who had been investigated and proven reliable for security purposes could work with top secrets.

With firm logic and a straight face, Bucky replied: "It is not necessary for me to be cleared in order to trust myself. I already know my own top secrets."

Knowledge of such "top secrets" as the domes had spread rapidly through the civilian world. The Department of Commerce ordered a dome to house the U.S. exhibit at the International Trade Fair in far-off Afghanistan. A single DC-4 plane carried all the parts for a dome to the city of Kabul. A single engineer went along to direct the construction. When the load was unpacked, the air buzzed with questions.

What were the Americans thinking of? How could the unskilled Afghan tribesmen who spoke no English put together this advanced piece of technology?

Bucky's design included a color code which made the job incredibly easy. The workmen had only one simple direction to follow. Bolt blue-ended parts to blue parts, red ends to red

The first radome, on top of Mt. Washington

Assembling the U.S. Pavilion for the International Trade Fair in Kabul, Afghanistan

parts. Within forty-eight hours, the aluminum tubes had all been bolted together and covered by a nylon skin.

The magical speed with which the dome went up stunned both natives and visitors. For weeks and months, laborers had been working on the Russian and Chinese Communist buildings and had yet to finish. Overnight, the Americans had created a palace that might have come out of a fairy tale. The Afghans approved wholeheartedly of this modern cousin to their traditional buildings, the rounded yurts, while the foreigners murmured admiringly about the grace, elegance, and strength of the dome.

The huge dome drew record-breaking crowds and pages of praise for America's technology. The Department of Commerce realized that the domes served a double purpose. They were superbly suited to house exhibits and were themselves an attractive exhibit or symbol of American "know-how." The government promptly ordered more and bigger domes for fairs and exhibitions everywhere. Fuller domes flew around the globe—Europe, Africa, Asia—to earn him a worldwide reputation.

There seems to be no limit to the usefulness of geodesic domes or the speed with which they can be put together.

The Kaiser Aluminum Company manufactured one for use as an auditorium in Honolulu. The day that construction started, Henry Kaiser flew from the mainland to Hawaii. He wanted to see the dome being put together. By the time he landed, it was too late. The dome was finished. Twenty-two hours after the parts had landed on the island, an audience of over one thousand people sat in the dome listening with pleasure to a concert by the Hawaiian Symphony Orchestra.

The finished pavilion at night, Kabul, Afghanistan

Children everywhere know and love Fuller's domes. Play-domes, small ones, went into mass production in 1957. Daily, children clamber over these in parks, school playgrounds, and their own backyards. They stretch both their minds and muscles as they swing from the bars, play King of the Mountain, or imagine themselves in a jungle.

A long, snaking train of railroad cars glides into a twelve-story-high dome in Louisiana. This dome is a plant for rebuilding railroad cars. A thousand different kinds of plants grow on different levels in the enormous greenhouse dome called the Climatron in St. Louis.

Banks, chapels, restaurants, homes, theaters. The domes are serving the people in countless ways. Thousands of domes dot the world today.

Bucky Fuller was a man who designed for tomorrow and tomorrow had finally arrived.

Children on a playdome in Albany, N.Y.

The exterior (above) and interior (below) of a Kaiser dome in Honolulu, Hawaii

12   At one time or another, every child starts a collection of some kind. Stamps, rocks, autographs or coins, perhaps. When Bucky Fuller was four years old, he chose to collect paper. Any and every scrap of paper that was written on by him, about him, or to him went into his collection. From a shoe box full of paper, the collection has grown to six tons of records stored now in the Science Center at Philadelphia. Papers are filed by the year in filing boxes; cans of film, tapes, and videotapes of lectures and interviews fill the shelves of a room. In still another room, masses of slides and architectural drawings are slowly being sorted out. His Chronofile is possibly the most complete record ever kept of a human life. Studying this model of one life, future historians may better understand the patterns or trends of what was happening to people around the world in the twentieth century.

In the year 1958, Bucky's Chronofile records a sharp swing upward in printed material by and about him. Thanks to the domes, people everywhere wanted to hear what R. Buckminster Fuller had to say. That year he took the first of his many trips around the world, delivering dozens and dozens of lectures along the way.

Domes made Bucky world-famous, yet he emphasizes that they were simply one result of the bargain he had made with himself years ago. He had hoped to discover the principles operating in the Universe and use them to make mankind a success. Instead of domes, Bucky points out that he could well have ended up with "flying slippers."

For Bucky, the design revolution had only just begun. He organized several companies to handle his many activities. Geodesics, Inc. handled the patents and farmed out the licenses for the domes. These licenses gave construction and other companies the right to manufacture domes. For every dome built, Bucky received a royalty of 5 percent.

Hundreds of thousands of dollars poured into his offices. Just as promptly, thousands and thousands of dollars poured out into

A geodesic restaurant in Woods Hole, Mass.

his research projects. The only use Bucky had for money was to buy materials and time for his work.

Money did buy for Bucky one very real pleasure. He used some of his new wealth to become the owner of the finest boat he could find. When Bucky sailed the sleek *Nagala* into the deep waters of Bear Island's harbor, he was a child whose Christmas dream had come true.

"Uncle Bucky, Uncle Bucky. It's Uncle Bucky."

The shrill welcoming cries of the children floated out from the shore across the water. Always, it seemed, there were children playing on Bear Island. First it had been the Fuller children, the caretaker Hardie's children, and the King cousins from Chicago. Now their children's children piled up pebbles on the beach, splashed in the water, and scattered outside the Great House for hide and seek. Allegra, married to film director Robert Snyder in 1951, had two little ones now: a daughter named Alexandra, and a son, Jaime. Bucky took great pleasure in them and the host of great-nieces and great-nephews.

Whether Bucky was their uncle or not, all the children seemed to regard him as one. He was one adult who never talked down to them, who never told them to run away and play.

"A child wants to understand the whole thing . . . Universe," says Bucky. "Children draw pictures with everything in them . . . houses . . . trees . . . and the sun AND the moon."

He points out that grownups then criticize and tell the child not to put the sun and the moon in the sky at the same time.

"But, the child *is* right! The sun and moon *are* in the sky at the same time."

Bucky believes firmly that a child is born competent and capable of treating large quantities of information right from the start. Then and now, Bucky gives a child's every question the most serious attention.

Bucky and his family in 1963; Allegra, Jaime, Robert Snyder and
Alexandra are in the front row, with Bucky and Anne behind

Bucky's home in Carbondale, Ill.

August on Bear Island recharged Bucky's energies for the year ahead. From being a college dropout, R. Buckminster Fuller had moved up to become a University Professor at Southern Illinois University. Carbondale, Illinois, became home base where he touched down briefly. The Fullers lived on the campus—in a small dome, of course—but Bucky Fuller traveled constantly, teaching students all across the country.

Some of these invitations to talk led Bucky to strange places. The Semantics Studies Group consisted of 140 members, all of them convicted criminals in San Quentin prison.

At seven o'clock in the morning, Bucky Fuller sat on a bare stage watching these young men with bowed heads filing in one by one to take a seat.

Bucky and Anne at home in Carbondale

What had prompted these men to invite him to speak? What should he say to such a group? What would concern them?

Bucky remembered his own mother's constant worry that her son would end up in the penitentiary some day. Only a tiny hair of luck separated him from them. Eyes closed, his hands held together in a steeple, he concentrated on reviewing with them every single thing that he knew. Like a Pied Piper of the mind, he led them down the paths that he had explored to understand Universe.

Suddenly, he realized that it was mid-afternoon. He had been talking for nearly *eight hours*. He stopped.

In a quick dash, the prisoners were jumping onto the stage. The men grabbed his hand, shaking it hard; they clapped him on the back.

"Bucky, this is the greatest day of my life," one called out.

The men jumped down from the stage, racing to the door. Within minutes, the room had emptied completely. It was already 3:30, time for the head count of prisoners which took place before locking up. If anyone missed the head count, he was placed in solitary confinement for a week. Yet every man there had risked that punishment. Not one would leave until Bucky had finished talking. Tears still come to Bucky's eyes when he recalls that moving tribute.

Almost as surprising was the call that came from Harvard University. Would R. Buckminster Fuller accept an appointment as the Norton Professor of Poetry? As a visiting professor, he would spend two months on the campus giving a series of lectures.

Bucky Fuller a poet? R. Buckminster Fuller had been labeled many things: an inventor, an architect, an engineer, a mathematician. But a poet?

Once a little girl had asked: "Bucky, why is the fire so hot?"

Bucky reminded her of the time when the tree from which the log came was growing in the sunlight and ended with, "what you see now is the sunlight, unwinding from the log."

Describing environment, he wrote:

> *Environment*
> To each must be
> All that is
> That isn't me.
>
> *Universe*
> In turn must be
> All that is
> Including me.
>
> The only difference between
> *Universe* and
> *Environment* is *me*—
> The experiencing observer.

If a poet can be defined as someone who puts things together, then Bucky has earned that title, too. Later, publishers agreed with Harvard when they printed his *Intuition*, a book-long poem.

Whatever the label, students jammed Bucky's lectures. Was there a grin on Bucky's face when he compared this stay at Harvard with his earlier ones? Forty-seven years ago he had been sent home from that campus in disgrace. Now he served as an invited, honored member of the faculty. He had been awarded medals and honorary doctor's degrees from more than a dozen universities. Bad Bucky Fuller who had failed to graduate with his class had come a long way. Bucky's busy pen added to his achievements. Five of his books were issued in 1963.

New evidence that same year pointed up the unique discoveries and importance of his Synergetics. While U.S. astronaut John Glenn sailed out into the vast new ocean of outer space, scientists with the new powerful electron microscope were exploring the tiniest form of life on earth, the virus. They examined the outside protein shells of viruses. What they found sent them to Fuller's books. The shape of one virus was identical with the officers' quarters dome in Korea. The chicken-pox virus matched the structure of the geodesic on top of Mt. Wash-

Bucky lecturing

ington. His radome in the Arctic was like an infectious hepatitis virus.

Bucky's mathematical formula for the design of the geodesic dome had predicted and explained perfectly the architectural structure of the protein shell surrounding many viruses.

On January 10, 1964, *Time* magazine put R. Buckminster Fuller on its cover. Like Fuller's inventions which were painted into the background, the portrait of Bucky was a modern fantasy. The artist could not resist turning Bucky's balding dome into a geodesic. Breaking up the top of Bucky's head into the famous tetrahedrons, he nevertheless got a good likeness. Bucky laughed at the result and wrote a letter to *Time* expressing his delight with the cover.

At sixty-nine, Bucky's face now had some lines etched into it. His crew-cut white hair had thinned. Light shining through it made it look like a fuzzy halo around the back of his head. Although he could hear some single sounds well enough, his hearing had failed. In crowds he stood with his head cocked like an expectant sparrow trying to strain out those sounds that he could still hear. But Bucky's bounce and eagerness to share ideas had not lessened one bit.

Bucky and his grandson, Jaime, on Bear Island in 1968

When his niece Kariska's school asked him to be the graduation speaker, he willingly squeezed in one more lecture. To the young graduates, Bucky presented his description of planet Earth.

"Young people are always wondering what it's like to be on a spaceship. . . ."

Bucky's answer to that question was to ask another question.

"Well, what *does* it feel like? Because that's what you're on. The earth is a very small spaceship hurtling through space. It's only eight thousand miles in diameter and the nearest star is ninety-two million miles away. . . . This spaceship is so superbly designed that we've had men on board here for about two million years reproducing themselves, thanks to the ecological balance . . . all the vegetation is breathing up all the gases needed by the mammals and all the mammals are giving off all the gases needed by the vegetation. . . ."

Bucky's phrase "Spaceship Earth" captured the imagination not only of those young graduates but also the imagination of the world. People use it commonly today. More importantly, our view of the earth, our planning and direction for the future, and our understanding of the universe have all been influenced significantly by this use of Bucky's concept.

A helicopter landing on the lawn put a dramatic end to Bucky's speech. He had to hurry away to the next talk. By plane, boat, and car Bucky continued giving lectures on an ever-more crowded schedule. He wrote articles for magazines and still found time to explore new designs. The list of patents to his credit grew longer: Aspension, Monohex, the Laminar Dome, the Star Tensegrity.

When Americans were chosen for the Dartmouth Conference, Bucky was asked to be a delegate. The Dartmouth Conference brought together leading American and Soviet citizens in fields ranging from science and medicine to literature. They discussed what nations must do for successful survival on earth. As private citizens, they could talk freely and frankly about any and all problems.

That August of 1964, the group met for six days in Leningrad, U.S.S.R. They sat in the huge, crystal-chandeliered ballroom of an old mansion. Each person had earphones so he could hear an instant translation of what was being said. On the last day, each side presented its thoughts about life in the future. The Americans, naturally, chose Bucky to give their views.

Through the morning Bucky sat, head cocked, listening to the Russian speaker. A thick black elastic band circled the back of his head and hooked on to the end of his glasses. It saved him from having to push his heavy glasses back up on his nose, and helped him to focus through the right part of his lenses. Bucky had the whole afternoon to present the American side. As always, he had no prepared speech. He stood up and began:

"I don't know why I'm talking to you here because you're all so ignorant."

Startled surprise. The murmurs buzzed more loudly around the room as the meaning of what he said dawned on the Russians. Bucky himself was a little surprised at what he had said. But he proceeded to think out loud.

"Many of you think of yourselves as scientists . . . you see a beautiful sunset . . . and you actually *see* the sun setting, going down. You've had four hundred years to adjust your senses since you learned from Copernicus and Galileo that the earth wasn't standing still with the sun going around it."

Bucky shook his head in mock despair.

"But you scientists still see the sun setting. And you talk about things being 'up' or 'down' in space when what you *really* mean is 'out' in space or 'in.'"

Da! Da! By this time, the Russians were laughing in agreement.

Bucky had serious points to make. Eyes closed as he concentrated deeply, Fuller talked for an hour and a half.

"We must recognize what we *don't know*. . . . Either war is

The Dartmouth Conference in Leningrad, 1964; Fuller is fourth from left at the table

obsolete or men are. . . . Man must be very responsible in the future. . . ."

At the end, the man who had spoken for the Russian side turned to an American editor. "The Americans win. No question about it. Mr. Fuller was magnificent."

With all his triumphs, with all his prizes and awards, Bucky Fuller still had no license to practice as an architect. To make contracts and build his structures, he needed a licensed architect. He took as his partner Shoji Sadao, a brilliant graduate of the Cornell School of Architecture. (The two men had become fast friends when Shoji worked on Bucky's geodesics at Cornell.) Fuller and Sadao, Inc., was the firm chosen to design the U.S. Pavilion for Expo '67, the Canadian World's Fair.

For anyone else, designing the pavilion might have been a full-time job. For Bucky, it was one more project to be squeezed into his whirlwind schedule. Every day he drank gallons of tea and worked twenty or more hours. When he finished, the plans looked like a math textbook. Instead of the usual pages of blueprints and drawings, there were tables and tables of figures.

"A 20-Story Bubble by Fuller to Hold U.S. EXPO '67 Display" was the headline telling the public what to expect.

Bucky's Bubble, a transparent geodesic dome, rose a spectacular 187 feet into the air to provide six million cubic feet of exhibit space. Thousands of separate plastic hexagons covered the steel frame. Because they could turn individually, these panels made a live, breathing skin for the dome. Electric motors programmed by a computer opened and closed these panels according to the weather. Some had valves to control the amount of fresh air inside. Others had light sensors which responded to the sun. As the sun rode through the sky, the sensors directed the raising and lowering of shades. Sometimes the shimmering dome was transparent, sometimes it was silver-colored. Lit up at night, the dome glowed like a jewel.

Every visitor who rode on the elevated monorail train passed directly through the Bubble. The exhibit, "Creative America," was displayed on a series of platforms set at different heights. Escalators linked the different platforms which filled the dome. While people might argue about the quality of the exhibits, there was no debate about the quality of the pavilion. The wit who called it "Buckminster Cathedral" was not far off the mark. It was truly one of the most beautiful creations of the human mind.

About a month after the opening of Expo '67, Bucky and Anne flew up to Montreal to see the fair. They walked through the dome slowly. What a wonderful fiftieth wedding anniversary present for them both to hear the awed, enthusiastic, and admiring comments of the fairgoers.

When they returned to New York, their pleasure came to an abrupt end. The taxi in which they were riding home crashed into the back of a truck. Both were thrown against the windows and bruised. A minor accident, everyone decided after they took stock of the damage.

Bucky and Jaime inside the U.S. Pavilion at Expo '67 in Montreal

Within days, it became clear, however, that something was terribly wrong. Anne, who had hit her head, suffered horrible headaches and dizzy spells. At the hospital, tests showed the damage—massive bleeding inside the brain. A leading surgeon ordered an operation immediately. No one knew whether the operation could repair the damage.

Would she live or die? Would she regain consciousness or remain an unseeing, silent vegetable for the rest of her days?

For Bucky, who had asked questions all his life, these were the most agonizing, unbearable questions he had ever faced. Without Anne, his loving partner of fifty years, the fame, success, and the respect of the world meant nothing.

In the end, the surgeon's skill, Anne's own inner strength, and Bucky's love were rewarded. Anne recovered completely.

13 Bucky Fuller still puzzled the world. At seventy-two surely he would sit back, slow down, and enjoy the fruits of his labor. After all, the domes were "perking along nicely," as Bucky put it, and they had earned for him a prize that could not be bought with money. The Harvard chapter of Phi Beta Kappa, the honor society, had voted him a membership with the right to wear the famous golden key. Bucky Fuller, however, persisted in working far out on the frontier.

He expects domes to be used as "environment valves" to cover whole sections of cities. For midtown Manhattan, he proposed a superdome to stretch from river to river and cover the area between 21st and 63rd streets. The dome would soar three-quarters of a mile above the Empire State Building but contain less steel than an ocean liner. It would be almost invisible.

What possible use could a "cover" be to a city?

Temperature and humidity could be controlled. The savings in energy costs alone would be tremendous. Additionally, the snow removal that costs New York City so much money each year would be eliminated. From the heated skin of the dome, melted snow would run off into gutters and be piped into reservoirs for future use instead of being wasted.

Despite the success of the domes, some things had not changed in this world. Bucky's proposal was too much like science fiction for the city officials, who refused to buy it.

Even more startling was his design for foldable buildings that could be used on the moon. Like exploding seed-pods, these would pop open to erect themselves, thus providing instant shelter.

"If I did not know better, I would swear that R. Buckminster Fuller was the figment of somebody's imagination, possibly my own," said one person.

A very real, very alive Bucky continued to circle the globe. He kept up his hectic pace of travel and work but became worried at one point about his flagging energy. Was age finally slowing him down? Or was it perhaps all that extra weight that

A composite picture shows how a dome would cover the midtown Manhattan area of New York City

he was carrying around? Too many banquets, too much rich food had made his stocky figure a very round one indeed.

Bucky solved his problem simply. Every day thereafter, for breakfast, lunch, and dinner, he ate only steak and applesauce. To keep track of time on his constant flights, he wore three watches. One was set at the time in his home office, one for the place in which he was at the moment, and the third for the place that he was going to.

In his travels, Bucky met a man whose vision matched his own. Matsutaro Shoriki, a Japanese multimillionaire, wanted Japan to make a really great contribution to the world. He felt, as Bucky did, that the greatest problem is how to house people and give them a standard of living that really means something. Mr. Shoriki hired Bucky to develop plans for a city of a million people.

Bucky tackled the colossal job very scientifically. He fed statistics into the computer, examined facts and figures. Each phase took months of study. There had been planned communities before, but nothing like what was emerging from Bucky's study.

His vast city would float like a ship on the waters of Tokyo Bay. Anchors would keep it from rolling and pitching. Although it might be connected to the land by bridge-ways, the floating city would be completely independent, providing all its own services, wasting nothing, recycling everything.

What shape did this floating city take? Naturally, it would be a tetrahedron, providing the greatest possible surface area for the space that it enclosed. The sloping outside surface would give occupants their own private terraced garden homes. Shopping centers and common-purpose areas would be located on the inside. Tennis, athletic fields, recreation areas would be on the top deck.

This city would start small, perhaps with two hundred thousand people. By adding tetrahedrons, just as a crystal does in

Model of Triton City, Fuller's proposed floating city

Nature, the city would grow to a height just under a mile and contain a million people.

Bucky has described this great dwelling machine as a "sort of large bookcase." Imagine the dwelling units (mass-produced, of course) raised and lowered mechanically to the terraces. It would be like placing boxes on a shelf. While parts such as the power plant would remain fixed, others could be detached to float elsewhere. Going on vacation, an occupant might remove his apartment and put it in one of those breakaway sections to sail around the world. The possibilities stretch endlessly.

Before the study could be completed, Mr. Shoriki died. When the U.S. government asked Bucky to complete the full design and make a model, he felt hopeful about his floating city. Such a gigantic project would require the cooperation of the federal as well as the state and local governments. And the city of Baltimore was considering anchoring one in Chesapeake Bay.

Unfortunately, the fall elections of 1968 brought a change in government. New officials scrapped the plans. Lyndon Baines Johnson, retiring from the Presidency, took the models of Triton City for his library in Texas. Although the project died, the idea lives on. Tourists at Expo '75 in Okinawa saw "Aquapolis," a small working prototype of a floating city. It offers one answer to the housing and environmental needs of the future.

More and more often, Bucky was expressing his concern about our environmental needs. One important fact had emerged from the charts which he kept. By harnessing technology and energy to use the world's resources, more people were living better than ever before. In 1900, only 1 percent of humanity had adequate shelter and food. By the middle of this century, over 40 percent enjoyed more physical comforts and conveniences in shelter, food, transportation, and communication than in all history.

With the population increasing constantly and resources decreasing, how was this possible?

By doing more with less, said Bucky's charts. For example,

farmers were producing more food from fewer acres and doing it with less labor.

In his own boyhood, the mechanics of living required a great many structures and outbuildings. Gradually, the woodshed became a furnace, the ice house became a refrigerator. Today bulky radio tubes have been replaced by tiny transistors. A communications satellite weighing about a ton carries more messages than 175,000 tons of transoceanic cable.

"I am absolutely convinced that we have enough," says Bucky. "Our planet earth can successfully support all humanity for generations to come. We do not have an energy crisis. We have a crisis of ignorance."

Bucky's World Game which he began in 1969 was designed to overcome this crisis of ignorance. The game includes an inventory of the world's resources and uses scientific means, including computers, to explore the efficient use of these. In Bucky's game, everybody wins, for the object is to help everyone live better than ever before. In workshop meetings each year, amateurs and experts together look for the critical path. When the world is ready to look for sensible solutions, the World Game will have information and strategies ready.

Always ready for new experiences, full of optimism and a zest for living, Bucky never could resist either a challenge or a joke. In Colorado, a seventy-two-year-old Bucky put on skis for the first time in his life. He maneuvered a bit on those long, awkward, curved slats.

"What do you think of it?" his host asked.

With a perfectly straight face, Bucky answered that he had unlocked the secret of the sport. After all, it was simply "angular valving of gravity."

In Canada, Bucky once shook a whole room full of dignified, important guests into laughter. At Carleton University, the fancy dinner with people in formal dress had gone on for a very, very long time. Introduced as a man who "operates spontaneously" and never prepares a speech, Bucky opened his remarks with: "The first thing I have to say spontaneously is that I have to leave for the men's room."

From Canada to Australia, to Greece, to Iran, to England, to Israel went Bucky, crisscrossing the United States in between. In 1970 alone, he delivered over eighty speeches. After a Fuller speech in India, the government leaders, much impressed, asked Bucky to design three new airports at New Delhi, Bombay, and Madras. Along the way that year, he picked up the Gold Medal of the American Institute of Architects, that same group that had rejected his offer of patents forty-one years ago. (The state of New York, too, recognized his genius, finally granting him an architect's license in 1974.)

Anne shared his pleasure in this award and shared, too, in his travels. The Delos Symposium held every summer combined both business and pleasure perfectly. Constantinos Doxiadis, a Greek city planner, organized these floating conferences. Distinguished thinkers sailed on a yacht through the Aegean visiting historic sites. In an exhilarating mix of past, present, and future, the group discussed solutions to world problems.

But always Bucky reserved August for Bear Island. That young boy who had invented a push-pull pole for his boat had grown up, but he still tinkered with better ways of rowing. One of his patents in 1970 was for a rowing device. A friend, Don Moore, built a prototype of this "Rowing Needle" and a picture shows Bucky testing it in the water at Bear Island.

Bucky on the prototype of the "Rowing Needle," Bear Island, 1970

The reservoir of ideas never ran dry. And the breakthroughs that proved Bucky's theories correct continued to arrive almost on a schedule. Tensegrity structures, frail-looking but tough, are another offshoot of Bucky's work in Synergetics. Contracting two words, tension and integrity, Fuller created a new one, tensegrity, to describe a principle of building relationships. He saw the possibility of having a spherical building in which the struts or "bricks" (the compression parts) did not touch one another anywhere. In this rounded structure, the compression struts are like islands, separate and alone. "Rubber bands" or tension parts interlaced keep the struts in place. The ends of each compression member connect only with the tension network at various points. In basic tensegrity structures, the spheric-tension network system is completely continuous. Fuller is convinced that all structures, properly understood, from the solar system to the atom, are tensegrity structures.

He found surprising behaviors in the tensegrity structures that he experimented with. If you just tighten one point in his tensegrity system, all the other parts of it tighten evenly. In 1949, Kenneth Snelson, a student of Bucky's, demonstrated a tensegrity system by building what he called a Tensegrity Mast. Ever since, Bucky had been looking for a way to put tensegrity principles to work. In theory, there was no limit to the uses; in practice, there were continuing problems.

Don Moore brought still another version of a tensegrity sphere to Bear Island in 1972. Fully relaxed, the tensegrity structure could be crumpled together without hurting it. It was much like a string net shopping bag which can be stuffed into a small space. This latest design introduced rectangular "door" and "window" sections while keeping the triangles which made the structure so fantastically strong. Moore threaded clothesline rope (the tension part) through short hollow rods (the compression parts) and tied knots. Finally, as the clothesline tensed, the jumbled heap of rods and rope blossomed into an erect sphere.

Bucky's niece Leslie Gibson and her husband, Dana, were there that memorable day. Dana Gibson recalls the look on

Assembly of a tensegrity sphere

Bucky's face when this sphere succeeded in standing up to all the pressures and rough handling given it. "There was an explosion of pleasure. . . . I imagine Newton must have looked like that when he was hit on the head with the apple."

Tensegrity spheres have a special characteristic. Incredibly light, their strength multiplies tremendously as they are made larger. Tensegrity structures are lighter-weight refinements of the rigid geodesic dome.

Another major event in 1972 was the Fullers' move to Philadelphia. Four colleges (Bryn Mawr, Haverford, Swarthmore, and the University of Pennsylvania) combined their resources to offer Bucky a place in the University City Science Center. Luring Bucky away from Illinois seemed like a great victory to the newspapers, which headlined his arrival: "Man of Tomorrow Is Ours Today."

Philadelphians got a good look at what the man of tomorrow had done in his seventy-seven years on earth when the Franklin Institute was host to an exhibit, "The Design Science of R. Buckminster Fuller." The show, prepared by the Museum of Science and Industry in Chicago and sent around the country, included an actual Dymaxion Car. The show opened to the public on March 1, 1974.

Fuller with a Tensegrity Mast made by Kenneth Snelson, 1949

Roped off by itself, the freshly painted black beauty drew the attention of two small boys.

"That's some car. Wow!"

"No, you dummy. That's a plane."

"Oh, yeah? Where are the wings?"

"Folded up somewhere, I bet."

A quick look around to see where the guards were and then both of them slipped past the ropes. On tiptoe they tried to see through the windows. Then they flopped down on their backs, sliding under the car to look at the underside. When the uniformed guard pulled them out from under, the boys had reached an agreement: "That's the kind of car *I* want."

Young people everywhere seem to want what Bucky offers, particularly his vision of how to make the world work.

"We must stop burning fossil fuels," Bucky warned the students at Buffalo in February 1975. In a week-long series of lectures, he developed this point.

Fossil fuels—coal and oil—might be called a fossil savings account. It's all right to use a little of it, but only as a self-starter to link in with the main engines of Universe. (Automobiles use storage batteries to power self-starters. These then start the main engines which in turn restock the storage batteries.)

If, however, you continue to draw out of the savings account, there is nothing left to live on. We should be using our energy "income." Like the interest in a savings account, it is constantly being added into the account. Energy income can be drawn from such sources as the sun, the tides, and the wind.

Since you can't put a meter on the wind, big business had ignored such an energy source. And, as Bucky says with a wry smile, "Sunlight has been called wealth only by poets."

But the sun doesn't always shine and the wind doesn't always blow. What do you do then? Why, you work as Bucky was working even then at designing windmills that can capture and store the power more efficiently.

Finally, there was an answer, too, for all the mathematicians who had been waiting almost "prayerfully" for Bucky's master work, the book explaining his geometry. Fifty years in the making, it seemed as if the book would never be completed. In E. J. Applewhite, Bucky found a friend who could work and rework the pages with him. It took the combined efforts of the two men and seven successive editors at Macmillan to get the book into print. Titled, simply, *Synergetics*, the book was hailed as the "distilled wisdom of a lifetime" when it was published in the spring of 1975.

There was scarcely time to celebrate this major event and no time to celebrate Bucky's eightieth birthday and fifty-eighth wedding anniversary. Once again, and as usual, Bucky was flying to a far part of the world, this time to an archaeological dig in Malaysia.

The party postponed until August turned into a triple celebration marking Allegra's birthday as well. It seemed particularly fitting that the party should be held in the house at Sunset, Maine, which had for years belonged to his brother, Wooly. The people who bought it after his death had lived in it through the sixties. When the house was again offered for sale, Bucky bought it.

Friends, relatives, and neighbors came streaming in for the party on that moonlit night. Jim Quinn who ran the mail-boat was there with his wife. Marian Billings, the postmistress at Sunset, Anne's sisters Hope and Lolly, members of the Hardie family—it was a good-sized crowd that had collected. Surrounded by those he loved best—Anne, Allegra, the two grandchildren Alexandra and Jaime—Bucky beamed constantly. Musicians were tuning up, the table was piled high with food.

His sister-in-law was urging a small boy to have some potato salad.

"It came from Bear Island."

"I know. I made it but I don't recommend it," the young boy's voice rose clearly above the noise of the crowd.

Bucky's niece Leslie smiled. Voices rose and fell, murmuring and remembering other days, other nights. ". . . remember that awful storm when Bucky bailed and bailed . . . that poem he used to read, 'Don't Shoot, Boys, The Poor Devils Are Dying. . . .' " Fiddles played and the caller sang out the tune for a square dance. Bucky never could resist an invitation to dance. His tapping feet did a jig. Time now to open the presents.

What kind of presents do you give to an explorer of mathematics, one who has also traveled more miles around the world than Marco Polo, Columbus, and Magellan combined?

A necktie, some beautiful shells, from Rosy a biography of their famous great-aunt Margaret Fuller. A grinning Bucky said each was just what he had wanted.

One night off and tomorrow Bucky would be back at work. The checklist of future projects drawn up by Ed Applewhite was already two pages long. There were mountains of letters waiting to be answered. Archaeologists in Mexico had found a relationship between his Synergetics and the positioning of the pyramids. Some mathematicians wanted to explore the teaching of Synergetics in regular school courses. Perhaps the tensegrity structures could be used as cable pylons for high-voltage electrical transmission nets?

Bucky Fuller was still exploring designs and solutions for the tomorrow that is coming. He wasted no time on memories of past triumphs. Did he perhaps have regrets or feel dismay when news of a fresh disaster came?

On May 21, 1976, the wire services flashed the shocking news: "DOME MEETS DOOM." Newspapers and television reported that the former U.S. Pavilion in Canada, renamed the Biosphere and housing ecology exhibits, had caught fire. Two welders working with torches to seal an opening had set off the fire. Although the plastic skin was fire-resistant, the torch flame striking directly on it had turned the plastic into a burning liquid. The dome became a blackened skeleton within minutes. Fifteen fire trucks and eighty-five firemen arriving just twenty minutes later could do nothing more than be sure the fire was out before they left.

Friends around the world called and wrote letters of sympathy to Bucky; strangers wept at the sight of the smoke-blackened steel frame that was left. Shocking as it was to others, Bucky simply expressed gratitude and relief that no one had been caught inside by the fire. Only the skin was destroyed; the dome itself survives unharmed. A stark frame for enclosing space, it remains a triumphant symbol of the true wealth that Bucky has uncovered for the world. By his definition, wealth is made up of two parts: energy which transforms and knowledge which always only grows. His discoveries have added immeasurably to man's knowledge and turned the energies of the universe to the advantage of all humanity, now and future.

Bucky outside his Expo '67 dome

Epilogue

On July 4, 1976, America celebrated its two hundredth birthday. That day mayors were reading proclamations, church bells were ringing everywhere. From coast to coast, militiamen were firing muskets, sailing ships were swooping up rivers, fife and drum corps were beating out "Yankee Doodle" as Americans re-created the past.

At the bottom of the Western Hemisphere, voices whooping loudly broke the still, white silence of Antarctica. American scientists who had come to study the polar region were taking a holiday, too. They slid in hair-raising toboggan runs down the curve of the huge geodesic dome which sheltered their colony.

Under the hot Florida sun, thousands of people poured through the gates of the Kennedy Space Center to see the new exposition, "Third-Century America." The logo, or emblem, of the fair showed a person with outstretched hands reaching into the future. The future was symbolized by a geodesic dome at the top of the round badge. Crowds moved from one display to another. Huge geodesic domes, fifteen in all, covered the displays.

In Philadelphia, the President of the United States opened the celebration with a speech. Firecrackers kept popping while sudden showers soaked the marchers in the day-long parade. A steady stream of people, young and old, poured into a dim, hot auditorium. The crowd waited patiently as the stage lights were adjusted one last time, the microphones tested for sound. The seventh annual World Game was ready to begin.

A small, chunky figure walking with a slight tilt was escorted on stage. His escort draped the wire around the speaker's neck and clipped the pocket microphone in place. There was a still, expectant silence.

"I'd like very much to excite in you an *awareness* . . . and a compunction *to act*. . . ." Bucky Fuller's voice picked up speed.

While so much of America was looking back at the past, Bucky Fuller typically talked of the future. The demands from students, businessmen, educators to hear more never stopped coming in to his office. Somehow, the stresses and strains on Bucky seemed to balance out. New improved hearing aids helped him, as did his grandson Jaime, who often accompanied him. When Bucky did not quite hear a question, Jaime at his side would carefully and clearly repeat it for him. At eighty-one, Bucky's body tired more quickly and he sometimes spent as much as six or seven hours in bed. Even then, his mind would come joltingly awake as numbers poured through his brain, pushing him to the edge of another discovery.

Students continued to discover in Bucky an optimism and faith that inspired them. Freshmen coming on the Wesleyan University campus in September of 1976 saw posters announcing his speech at Crowell Concert Hall. Anyone who missed that speech could catch another the next week at Town Hall in New York.

Running from October of 1976 through February of 1977 was a special exhibit at the Cooper-Hewitt Museum in New York. The title was "Man Transforms." Leading architects and designers from all over the world had been invited to demonstrate the ways in which man transformed his environment. Bucky Fuller designed the exhibit in the handsome library of the old Carnegie mansion, home now of the museum.

School children trooping through the exhibits stopped short at the entry to the library. Where to look first? At the posters? At the geometric solids with rolling strips of cloth that danced over their heads? Or at the models displayed out in the open, inviting one to touch them? Through the small doorway in the little room off the library, a ten-minute film unrolled. Bucky Fuller himself was on the screen talking directly to them, unfolding his search for Nature's single system of structuring.

He confidently predicted that anyone who studied the exhibit and read the book, *Synergetics*, would come to agree with him about the cosmic significance of Synergetics. In the papers that a visitor could take home to read, Bucky noted, ". . . so, too, will a very surprised body of academic scientists." With typical Fuller enthusiasm, he urged the reader on:

> And you, too, as I have, can have the fun of beating them to it. The Synergetic bridge spanning the chasm between the humanities and sciences is now open for traffic, no toll to pay and a glorious view all the way.

Born in the nineteenth century with deep roots in America's past, R. Buckminster Fuller has kept his face turned firmly to the future. He is a living, visible link between America's past and her hopeful future. In his passionate, lifetime commitment to helping all men everywhere, he represents the best of the American dream.

Bibliography

Of the many books and articles dealing with Fuller and his work, the following were particularly useful in the preparation of this book. Books marked with an asterisk (*) are especially appropriate for young people.

ABOUT R. BUCKMINSTER FULLER

Applewhite, E. J. *Cosmic Fishing: An Account of Writing* Synergetics *with Buckminster Fuller*. New York: Macmillan Publishing Co., 1977.

Ben-Eli, M., ed. "Buckminster Fuller Retrospective." *Architectural Design* (London), December 1972, p. 747.

"The Dymaxion American." *Time*, January 10, 1964, p. 46.

Farrell, Barry. "The View from the Year 2000." *Life*, February 26, 1971, p. 46.

————. "R. Buckminster Fuller" (Interview). *Playboy*, February 1972, p. 59.

* Hatch, Alden. *Buckminster Fuller: At Home in the Universe.* New York: Crown Publishers, 1974.

Kenner, Hugh. *Bucky: A Guided Tour of Buckminster Fuller.* New York: William Morrow & Co., 1973 (hardcover and paperback).

————. "Bucky Fuller and the Final Exam." *The New York Times Magazine*, July 6, 1975, p. 10.

McHale, John. *R. Buckminster Fuller.* New York: George Braziller, 1962.

* Marks, Robert W. "Planet Earth: Buckminster Fuller's Hometown." *1971 Britannica Yearbook of Science and the Future*, p. 338.

* Rosen, Sidney. *Wizard of the Dome: R. Buckminster Fuller, Designer for the Future.* Boston: Little, Brown, & Co., 1969.

Tomkins, Calvin. "In the Outlaw Area" (Profile). *The New Yorker*, January 8, 1966, p. 35.

"The World of Buckminster Fuller." *The Architectural Forum*, January–February 1972, p. 49.

BY R. BUCKMINSTER FULLER

And It Came to Pass—Not to Stay. New York: Macmillan Publishing Co., 1976.

* *Buckminster Fuller to Children of Earth*. Garden City, N.Y.: Doubleday & Co., 1972.

The Dymaxion World of Buckminster Fuller. In collaboration with Robert W. Marks. New York: Reinhold, 1960. (Garden City, N.Y.: Anchor Press, 1973, paperback)

Earth, Inc. Magnolia, Mass.: Peter Smith, Publisher, 1973. (Garden City, N.Y.: Anchor Press, 1973, paperback)

Education Automation: Freeing the Scholar to Return to His Studies. Carbondale: Southern Illinois University Press, 1963. (Garden City, N.Y.: Anchor Press, 1963, paperback)

* *Ideas and Integrities*. Englewood Cliffs, N.J.: Prentice-Hall, 1963. (New York: Collier Books, 1969, paperback)

Intuition. Garden City, N.Y.: Doubleday & Co., 1973. (Garden City, N.Y.: Anchor Press, 1973, paperback)

Nine Chains to the Moon. Carbondale: Southern Illinois University Press, 1963. (Garden City, N.Y.: Anchor Press, 1971, paperback)

No More Secondhand God and Other Writings. Carbondale: Southern Illinois University Press, 1963. (Garden City, N.Y.: Anchor Press, 1971, paperback)

Operating Manual for Spaceship Earth. Carbondale: Southern Illinois University Press, 1969. (New York: Touchstone/ Clarion, 1970, paperback)

Synergetics: Explorations in the Geometry of Thinking. In collaboration with E. J. Applewhite. New York: Macmillan Publishing Co., 1975.

Untitled Epic Poem on the History of Industrialization. Charlotte, N.C.: Jonathan Williams, 1962. (New York: Touchstone/Clarion, 1971, paperback)

Utopia or Oblivion: The Prospects for Mankind. New York: Bantam Books, 1969, paperback. (Woodstock, N.Y.: Overlook Press, 1973; hardcover reprint of original 1969 edition)

RELATED READING

* Kondo, Herbert. *Adventures in Space and Time: The Story of Relativity.* New York: Holiday House, 1966.

* Ravielli, Anthony. *An Adventure in Geometry.* New York: Viking Press, 1957.

* Rogers, William G. *What's Up in Architecture: A Look at Modern Building.* New York: Harcourt, Brace, & World, 1965.

Index